Manned Spacecraft to Mars and Venus

About the Book

Unmanned probes studying Mars and Venus are preparing the way for manned interplanetary flight. In this appealing book the well-known aerospace writer Walter B. Hendrickson, Jr., gives an inside view of how these flights will be planned. Far more than human daring is involved in their being carried out successfully, he shows. Those who are skeptical about space travel will learn here how precise scientific planning can work the same magic in probing the outer planets that enabled American astronauts to step onto the moon.

IN PLANETARY ORBIT: This depicts a spacecraft in orbit around either Mars or Venus. (Courtesy General Dynamics/Astronautics)

HOW IT WORKS:

MANNED SPACECRAFT TO MARS AND VENUS
HOW THEY WORK

By Walter B. Hendrickson, Jr.

G. P. PUTNAM'S SONS   NEW YORK

Copyright © 1975 by Walter B. Hendrickson, Jr.
All rights reserved. Published simultaneously in
Canada by Longman Canada Limited, Toronto.
SBN: GB-399-60928-8
SBN: TR-399-20438-5
Library of Congress Catalog Card Number: 74-16627
PRINTED IN THE UNITED STATES OF AMERICA
12 up

Contents

Foreword **9**

Acknowledgments **11**

1 Charting the Course **13**

2 Power to the Planets **25**

3 Getting Ready **37**

4 Convoy to Mars **53**

5 Exploring Mars **73**

6 Down to Venus **89**

7 Stopover at Mercury **101**

8 Return to Earth **111**

Index **123**

MANNED SPACECRAFT TO MARS AND VENUS

Foreword

From the time people first began to think about travel to other worlds it was obvious that some kind of ship was needed for the trip. At first it was thought that a sailing ship or a cart pulled by birds could make the journey. For example, the first science-fiction story, *Vera Historia* ("True History") written by Lucian of Samosata, a second-century A.D. Greek, tells of a ship blown to the moon in a storm.

As more knowledge of space was gained, the ideas of what interplanetary spacecraft should be became more realistic. Astronomers discovered that the moon is an average of 238,000 miles from Earth and the nearest planets are millions of miles farther away. Obviously, a spaceship would have to carry food and water for this long journey.

Early balloonists discovered that the air thinned out rapidly as they floated up to altitudes several miles above the earth. Later high-altitude rockets showed that Earth's atmosphere practically disappeared above 500 miles. Now it was clear that a spaceship would have to carry its own air as well as food and water.

Also, the spacecraft needed an engine which could work as well in the vacuum of outer space as in the atmosphere. Science-fiction writers have suggested rockets, huge cannon, and antigravity for launching spaceships. So far, however, the rocket is the only one of the three that has proved practical for space travel.

Now, while Project Apollo has proved that man can journey to the moon, explore it, and return safely to Earth, unmanned probes are studying Mars and Venus. These spacecraft are preparing the way for manned interplanetary flights, just as unmanned moon probes led the way to the moon. Before men journey to Mars and Venus, however, larger and more advanced spacecraft will be needed. This book is the story of those spacecraft.

Acknowledgments

The story of manned spaceflight to Mars and Venus would not be complete without photographs to illustrate the parts described in the book. For these credit goes to: the National Aeronautics and Space Administration, Atomic Energy Commission, Ling-Temco-Vought, Inc., Electro-Optical Systems, Inc., Lockheed Missiles and Space Company, McDonnell-Douglas, Space Division and Oceans Systems Operations of North American Rockwell, Grumman Aircraft, Graphic Films Corp., General Dynamics Astronautics, Westinghouse, Martin-Marietta, Boeing Aircraft, and Movie Newsreels Co.

LIFT-OFF: A manned flight to the planets would begin with a scene like this launch of a Saturn V carrying an Apollo spacecraft. (NASA Photo)

1 Charting the Course

Eventually man will fly to the nearest planets, Mars and Venus—maybe in the next decade, maybe in the next century. Much of the preliminary work has already begun. The first step in preparing for a voyage to the planets, as with any trip, is to chart the course.

Mars will be the first planet visited because astronauts can at least survive on its surface with space suits. On the surface of Venus, by contrast the temperatures are near 1,000° F—hot enough to melt lead. In fact, several of the Russian space probes that have parachuted into Venus' thick, churning atmosphere have been crushed.

With such conditions men will not be setting foot on Venus on the first interplanetary flights—if indeed they ever do. However, a manned expedition could take a close look at Venus either on a flyby or from an orbit around the planet. The astronauts with the more elaborate equipment available to them could probably learn more than unmanned probes can. This visit to Venus could come as a bonus on the return from Mars.

Like the unmanned probes, it will be best if the manned Mars mission arrives at Mars when that planet is closest to Earth. Astronomers call it opposition because at that time Mars is on the opposite side of Earth from the sun. At opposition the reports from the Mars expedition will not have to travel over so great a distance to reach Earth.

Oppositions of Mars and Earth occur every twenty-five to twenty-six months. The distance between the two planets at opposition varies over a fifteen- to seventeen-year cycle. The last really close opposition was on August 10, 1971, when Mars was only 35,000,000 miles from Earth, the closest it ever comes. Since then the two planets have been farther and farther apart at each opposition.

This increase in distance will continue until February 25, 1980, when Mars and Earth will be 62,600,000 miles apart. After that the distances will decrease until July 10, 1986, when the two planets will be within 37,600,000 miles of each other.

This cycle of oppositions is convenient since the National Aeronautics and Space Administration (NASA) will not be ready to begin final preparation for the manned flight before 1980 at the earliest. The Russians probably will not be ready for a manned interplanetary flight any earlier either.

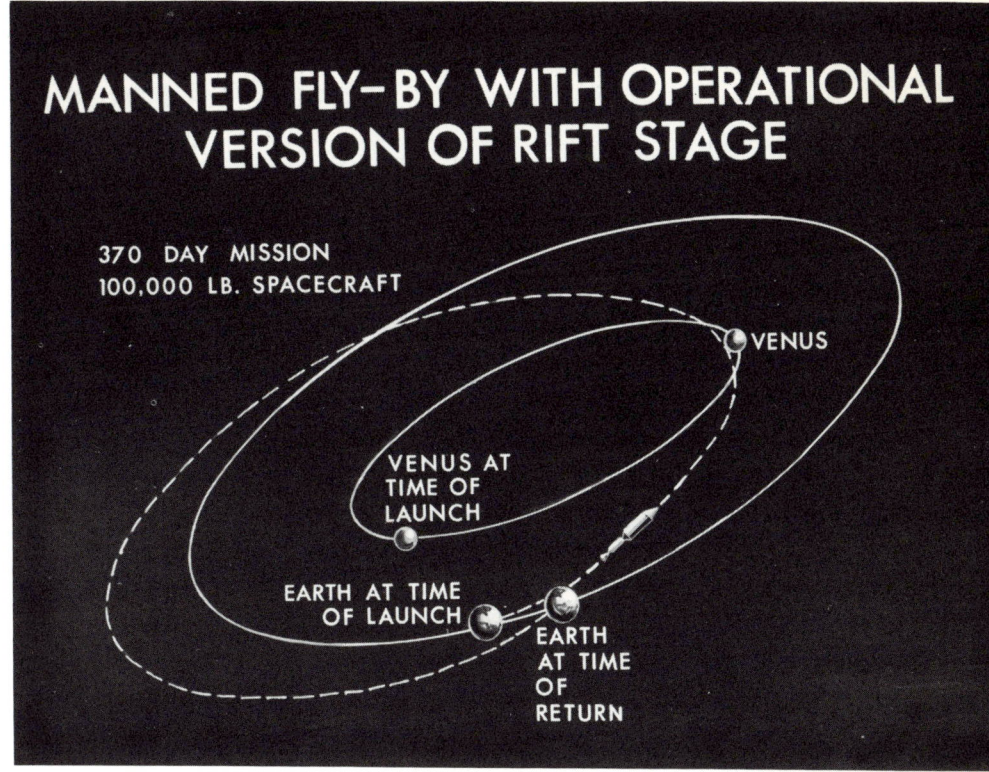

VENUS FLY-BY: The diagram shows the course a manned nuclear-powered spacecraft would take on a Venus fly-by. RIFT stands for Reactor In-Flight Tests. (NASA Photo)

Of course, the manned flight to Venus must also arrive at that planet when it is close to Earth. Astronomers call this inferior conjunction because Venus is then between Earth and the sun. These inferior conjunctions come every twenty-one months with a really close one every eight years. The first very close inferior conjunction of Venus at which a manned spacecraft could reach that planet is in September, 1983. At that time Earth and Venus will be within about 25,000,000 miles of each other.

Like the Apollo spacecraft, the manned interplanetary spacecraft will probably spend most of its flight coasting through space. Its large main rockets will be fired only when it needs a change in speed. The rest of the time the crew will use only smaller steering jets to keep their antenna lined up with Earth.

The first burst of power for the interplanetary spacecraft will come when it is launched into a parking orbit around Earth. Actually, several booster rockets will probably be used to put modules (sections) of the Mars ship into orbit. These modules will then be docked together in space for the Mars trip.

The interplanetary spacecraft will make its greatest increase in speed when it goes from the parking orbit into its flight to the target planet. Its main rocket will be used again at least three more times: to go into orbit around the target planet, to leave this orbit for a return to Earth, and to go into orbit around Earth. Other short bursts of power may also be needed for course corrections.

Some scientists have suggested that the first manned

flights to the planets, like the unmanned ones, should start with a flyby. However, in 1963 Dr. Krafft A. Ehricke, director of Advanced Studies at General Dynamics Astronautics, suggested that it would not be too much more difficult to orbit Mars on the first mission. A short visit to the surface of Mars might even be included on this mission.

One reason orbiting Mars is almost as easy as a flyby is that on a flyby the path (trajectory) of the spacecraft must be carefully plotted so that it will return to Earth after its flyby. This would cut down on the number of opportunities at which the spacecraft could be launched.

A mission to orbit a planet would only have to be launched in time to reach its destination when that planet was closest to Earth. The expedition could then wait in Mars orbit until a window occurred for a flight back to Earth.

A manned interplanetary spacecraft, like an unmanned space probe, must take a long, curving path through space to its target planet. It is impossible for any spacecraft, no matter how fast it can travel, to go straight from one planet to another. This is because the planets are all orbiting the sun in the same direction, each at several thousand miles per hour.

These speeds offset the pull of the sun's gravity, which affects everything in the solar system, including spacecraft. Each planet also has its own gravity which pulls on anything that comes near the planet.

To reach Mars, a spacecraft must speed up at least 8,045.24 miles per hour as it heads away from its parking orbit 186 miles above Earth. This speed, added to the 19,090.4 miles per hour at which it was traveling in the parking orbit, will send the spacecraft hurtling away from Earth at 27,135.6 miles an hour.

As the spacecraft heads out toward Mars, the gravity of the sun will gradually be slowing it down. By the time it reaches Mars, about 259 days after leaving Earth, it will be traveling slower than that planet. So the spacecraft will have to increase its speed to 4,090.8 miles per hour to go into a high orbit around Mars. To go into an orbit closer to the planet, the spacecraft will have to speed up still more to offset the greater pull of gravity.

If it did not go into orbit, the spacecraft would drop back toward Earth's orbit, but Earth might not be in position to meet it. For this reason the spacecraft will wait some time after going into Mars orbit before heading home. To save the most propellant (rocket fuel) on the return trip, the spacecraft would have to spend 455 days orbiting Mars. During this time Mars will have traveled nearly two-thirds of its way around the sun, and Earth will have circled the sun about one and a quarter times.

At the end of this time the spacecraft would increase its speed to 8,181.6 miles an hour heading out of orbit in the opposite direction from the way Mars is circling the sun. The spacecraft will then start dropping back toward Earth.

After another 259 days the spacecraft would again reach Earth. Upon its return the spacecraft would be traveling faster than Earth and would have to slow down to 17,448.3 miles per hour to get back into the Earth orbit, which it left some 2.66 years after the flight to Mars began.

Both the departure of the Mars ship from parking orbit and its return to that orbit will take place over the sunny side of Earth. So the public will have to be content with watching the arrival and departure of the Mars expedition on television. However, when a manned spacecraft leaves for Venus, some people on the night side of Earth will see a bright starlike light appear in the sky as the spacecraft's rockets begin to push it on its way.

The Venus-bound ship will accelerate to at least 25,289 miles per hour heading in the opposite direction from the way Earth travels around the sun. This will cause the spacecraft to begin dropping sunward. By the time it reaches Venus, 146 days later, the spacecraft will have been speeded up so much by the pull of the sun's gravity that it will have to slow down to 13,249.9 miles per hour to go into a high orbit around Venus.

As on the Mars mission, the spacecraft will have to wait in orbit around Venus until that planet and Earth are again in the right position for the trip home. To save as much fuel as possible, the spacecraft would have to wait in orbit around Venus 468 Earth days.

During this time Venus will have circled the sun twice and rotated on its axis almost two times. Venus takes 224.7007 Earth days to circle the sun while it rotates backward (from east to west) once every 243 Earth days. Meanwhile, the more sedate Earth will have gone around the sun one and a quarter times.

At the end of this long wait the spacecraft would start for home by increasing its speed to at least 4,249.9 miles per hour. This would put the spacecraft on a path that would bring it back to Earth in 146 days. When the spacecraft reaches Earth, the ship will increase its speed to 23,400 miles per hour returning to the orbit 186 miles above Earth, which it left 2.08 years before.

These long flights are called synodic missions. The visits to Mars and Venus could be made in much less time, but this would take more propellant. However, this fuel weight could be offset by a savings in other "consumables" (air, food, water, etc.). A shorter flight would also mean that the crew would be exposed to the hazards of space such as radiation, meteorites, and weightlessness for less time. This, in turn, would result in a weight savings since less equipment would be needed to protect the astronauts from these hazards. Of course, a whole new flight path with different launch windows would have to be calculated for a faster flight.

Just a little more speed would make a lot of difference in the time needed for the flight. For example, if the spacecraft left its orbit around Earth at 27,272 miles per hour—just 136.36 miles per hour faster—it would reach Mars in 200 days. This speed would be enough to carry the spacecraft on beyond Mars. So the spacecraft would have to slow down to 4,090.8 miles per hour to go into orbit around Mars.

If the expedition were prepared to travel home as fast as it traveled to Mars, it would only have to wait for 50 days before starting its return to Earth. It would then head away from its orbit around Mars at 13,636 miles per hour and begin to drop back toward the sun, reaching Earth in 200 days.

At the end of this flight the spacecraft would be hurtling toward Earth at 27,272 miles per hour. It would then have to slow down to 19,090.4 miles per hour to return to a parking orbit around Earth. The entire flight would take 450 days, almost half the time of the synodic mission.

The reason the spacecraft would be traveling so fast on its return to Earth is that on the way back from Mars it swings in as close to the sun as the orbit of Venus. During this close approach to the sun that body's gravity gives the spacecraft an extra boost in speed, known as a gravity assist.

If the spacecraft cut its stay time at Mars by ten days, it could flyby Venus on the way back to Earth. The gravity of Venus would slow the spacecraft somewhat, making the mission take as long as a synodic mission to Mars. There would, however, be the added bonus of the Venus flyby. Since the spacecraft would return to Earth more slowly after the Venus flyby, it would need less fuel than if it had visited only Mars. This will give an economy-minded space program planner a sort of two-for-one sale.

The astronauts will probably not be able to solve all the mysteries of Venus in a quick flyby, so a later mission could be sent to orbit Venus. As on the Mars trip, just a little more speed would save a lot of time.

Leaving Earth at the same speed as the expedition to Mars, but in the opposite direction, the spacecraft would reach Venus in about 140 days. It would then have to slow down to 13,249.9 miles per hour to go into orbit around

Venus. The spacecraft would then have to wait there just one month for a window to open for a quick return to Earth. The craft would then head back toward Earth at 25,226.60 miles per hour.

On its 250-day return flight from Venus the spacecraft would loop out beyond Earth and come in toward the night side of Earth at 27,272 miles per hour. The craft would then slow down to 19,090.4 miles per hour, returning to the orbit it left 420 days earlier.

If the Venus expedition left at just the right time and speed, its flight could include the added bonus of a stopover at Mercury. This two-planet mission is sometimes called a Bikini mission. Special insulation will be needed for this side trip because Mercury is only 36,000,000 miles from the sun. This gives the sunny side of Mercury, and anything near the planet, a heat of 650° F.

This temperature would be high enough to melt the hull of the spacecraft if it were made of aluminum! To prevent this, the outer hull of a Mercury-bound spacecraft will be made of Inconel X, a steel alloy which was used in the hull of the X-15 rocket plane. This metal can withstand temperatures from $-300°$ F to $1,200°$ F. A liquid nitrogen cooling system, similar to that used on the X-15, could take care of any heat that penetrates this hull.

Leaving Earth at 26,916.4 miles per hour, the expedition will reach Venus in 82 days. The astronauts will then spend about 68 days examining Venus from orbit while waiting for the launch window when they will be in position to leave for Mercury. The expedition will then start off on a 41-day trip to Mercury at 12,478 miles per hour.

After the Bikini mission goes into orbit around Mercury, a landing expedition could be sent down to explore a site on the surface of that planet. About 41 days will be spent exploring Mercury while that planet moves into inferior conjunction with Earth. The expedition will then leave for home at 14,672 miles per hour. The flight back will take 85 days, bringing the expedition back to Earth after 408 days in space.

During the return flight from Mercury the tug of the sun's gravity will have slowed the spacecraft down to 13,192 miles per hour. So it will have to speed up to 19,090 miles per hour to return to its parking orbit above Earth.

Because of the long duration of interplanetary flights, the first expeditions to Mars and Venus will be made by at least two spacecraft. In this way if one spacecraft should become disabled, its crew can be brought home by the sister spaceship.

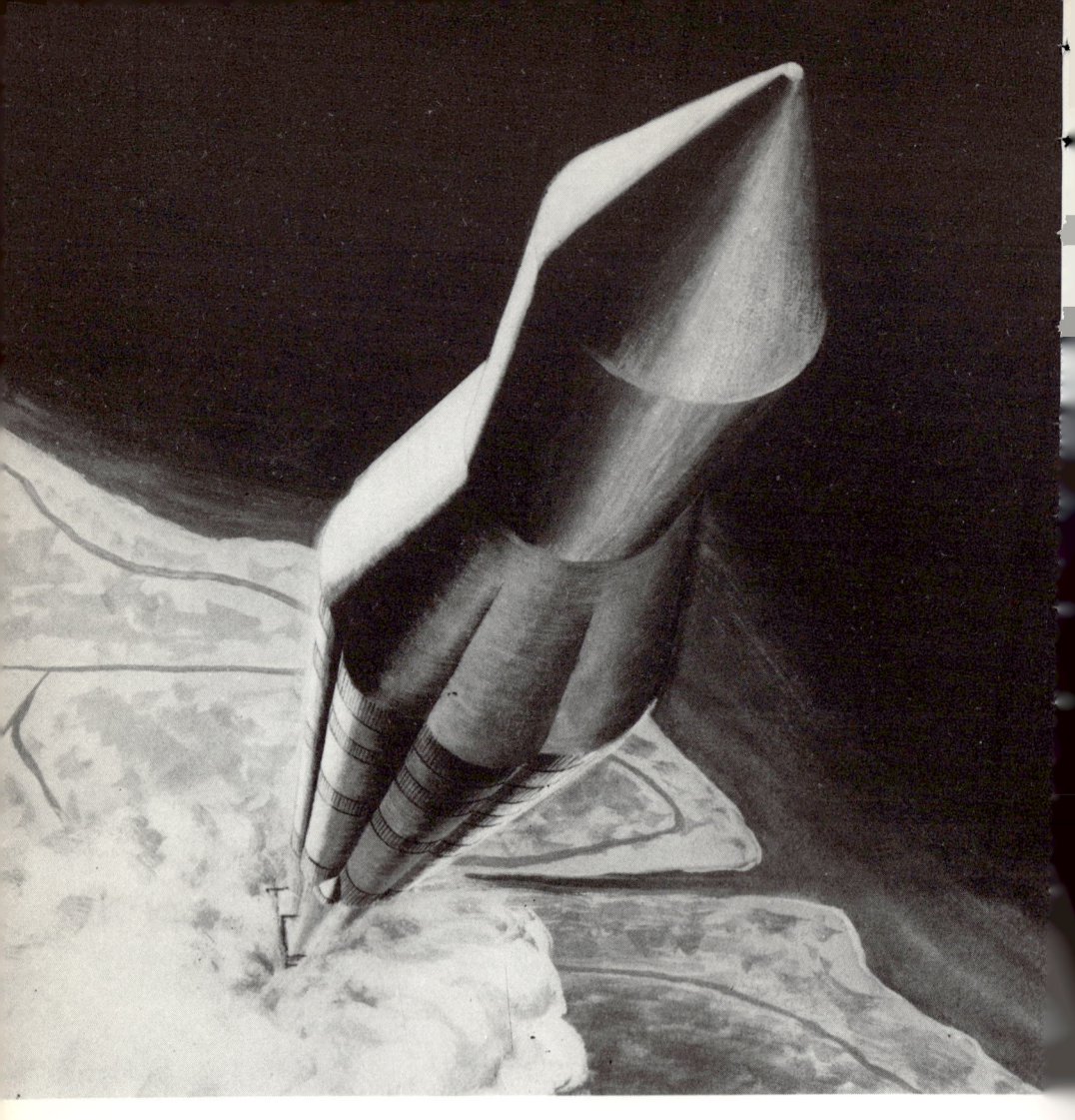

NOVA LAUNCHING: An artist's concept shows a giant NOVA rocket being launched into orbit from Cape Kennedy. (General Dynamics/Astronautics)

2 Power to the Planets

NASA has determined that a crew of twelve people, six on each spacecraft, will be needed to perform all the tasks that will arise during the flight. Besides exploring the planets and the space between them, the astronauts will have to be prepared to handle any emergencies that might confront them. They will have to be able to repair any equipment that malfunctions and to treat any injury or illness among the crew members.

If a spacecraft which could leave for the planets with six men and return with twelve, if necessary, were powered by liquid hydrogen and liquid oxygen, as were the Apollo spacecraft, it would weigh 6,400,000 pounds when fully fueled and ready to leave Earth orbit. Even the world's largest rocket, the Saturn V, can boost only 240,000 pounds into Earth orbit.

When plans were first being formulated for the Apollo moon landing, NASA engineers considered a rocket that would be more than three times as powerful as the Saturn V. This huge rocket, called the Nova, could land the entire Apollo spacecraft, not just the lunar module, on the moon. It could also place 1,000,000 pounds into Earth orbit.

Even with the Nova, seven launches would be needed to assemble a chemically fueled interplanetary spacecraft—six Novas and one Saturn V. Besides, while tripling the power of the Saturn V, the Nova would also triple the size, fuel requirements, noise, and the cost.

A better solution would be to find a more efficient rocket engine for the interplanetary spacecraft. The key to improving a rocket's performance comes from Sir Isaac Newton's Third Law of Motion: "For every action there is an equal and opposite reaction." It is the action of the escaping exhaust gases that creates the reaction that drives the rocket forward. To improve the performance of a rocket, one must increase the speed of its exhaust. This can be done either by raising the temperature of the exhaust or by using a lighter propellant.

Chemically fueled rockets already operate at as high temperatures as they can. In fact, this temperature of $4,040.6°$ F is so high that liquid-fueled rocket engines would melt if not cooled by circulating the fuel around the outside of the motor before injecting it into the combustion chamber. Also, liquid hydrogen with liquid oxygen is the lightest possible combination of chemical rocket propellants.

Some means of powering a rocket other than the combus-

SOLAR-HYDROGEN ROCKET PROTOTYPE: Technicians at Edwards Air Force Base, California, prepare a prototype of the SOHR for testing. Arrow indicates the rocket's nozzle. (Electro-Optical Systems, Inc.)

tion of chemical propellants must be used if the interplanetary rocket is to have a more efficient engine than those now in use. This could come from harnessing either the power of the atom or the power of the sun. Both nuclear rockets and solar rockets have had static (nonflying) tests.

A prototype of a solar-powered rocket was tested at the Air Force's Rocket Propulsion Laboratory at Edwards Air Force Base, California, in 1963. This is the **SOHR** (*SOlar Hydrogen Rocket*), developed by Electro-Optical Systems. The **SOHR** uses a 40-foot-wide, dish-shaped solar reflector to focus the rays of the sun on a 4.8-inch-wide can containing tightly coiled pipes filled with liquid hydrogen, the lightest of all liquids. The concentrated rays of the sun heat the hydrogen to around 3,500° F causing it to rush out the rocket nozzle.

The **SOHR** is so efficient that it can carry eleven times as much payload as a chemical rocket. The only trouble is that the solar rocket has an extremely low thrust. The test model of the **SOHR** developed less than 1 pound of thrust. More advanced **SOHR**'s are expected to develop up to 10 pounds of thrust. Obviously, this is not enough power to boost even a small spacecraft off the surface of Earth—but it could be used to depart from parking orbit.

In spite of this head start, a **SOHR**-powered spacecraft would take ten times as long to reach its destination as would a chemically powered rocket. This means that the **SOHR** rocket could not be used for the main drive of a manned interplanetary spacecraft. However, the **SOHR** would be very useful for steering jets since it uses so little fuel that it can keep running throughout the entire flight.

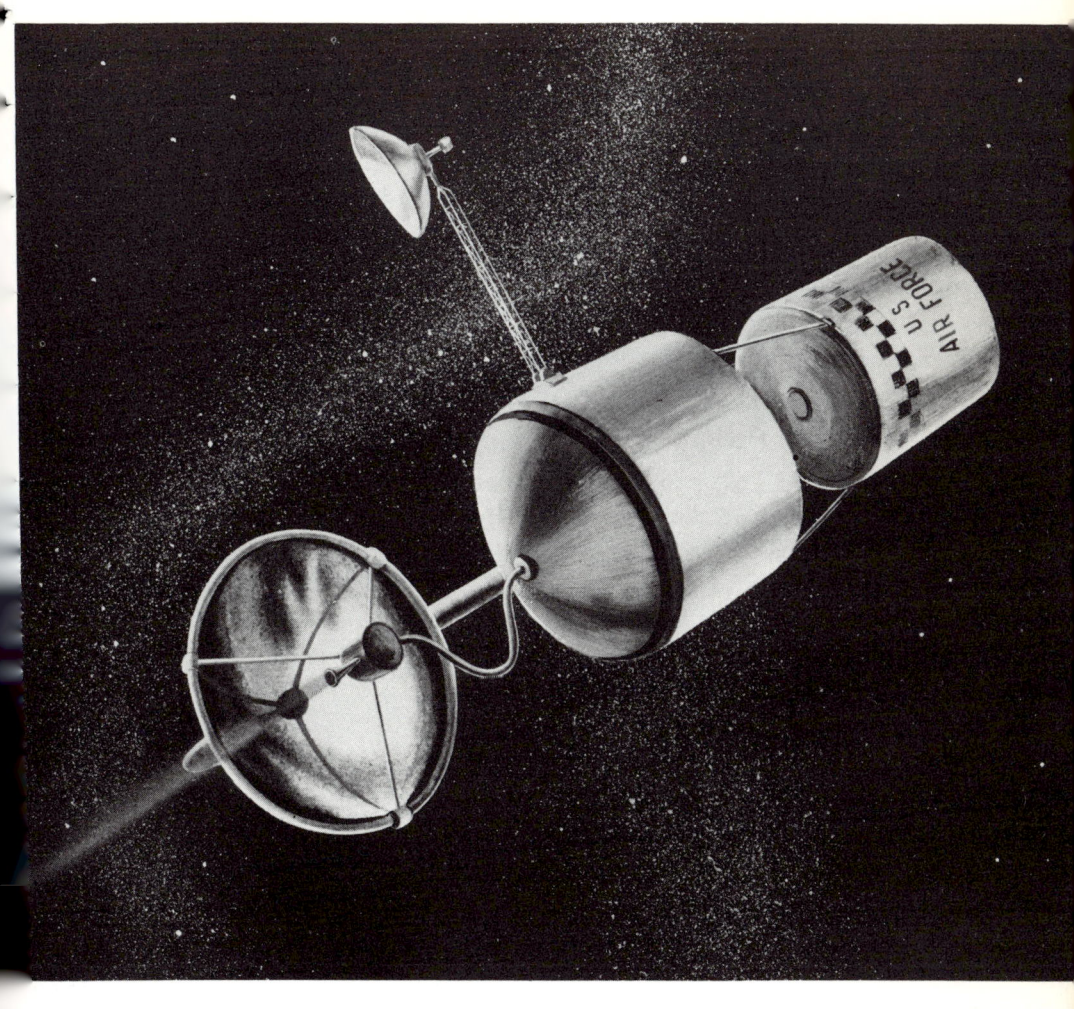

SUN ROCKET: This artist's concept shows a SOHR-powered spacecraft in flight. (Electro-Optical Systems, Inc.)

A solid-core nuclear rocket will be needed for the main drive of the interplanetary spacecraft. A nonflying prototype of such a power system, the NERVA (*N*uclear *E*ngine *R*ocket *V*ehicle *A*pplication) was developed by NASA in a joint program with the Atomic Energy Commission (AEC) which began in 1962.

Dr. Wernher Von Braun described the NERVA to the Senate Committee on Aeronautical and Space Science on August 5, 1969: "The engine consists essentially of a carbon moderated uranium reactor with a lot of little channels leading into the reactor. When the reactor goes critical, it assumes a white hot temperature. Liquid hydrogen back here heats up. Due to the fact that hydrogen gas is very light, the exhaust velocity is much higher than that of an exhaust from hydrogen combustion.

"As a result, such a nuclear engine gives us very good fuel economy, the 'specific' impulse (which is a measure of fuel economy of a rocket engine) is about twice as good as that of the chemically powered hydrogen-oxygen stages of the Saturn which boosted the Apollo spacecraft to the Moon."

The United States is forbidden by treaty from testing a nuclear rocket in the atmosphere. Besides, the nuclear rocket's exhaust would probably spread dangerous radiation in the atmosphere. For this same reason nuclear engines also will not be used to land on any other planets. In space, however, the radiation of the engines would be a minor matter compared to the natural sources of radiation there.

The walls of the spacecraft that protect the astronauts from the usual radiation in space will also protect them

NERVA ROCKET: A technician examines the nozzle of a test model of the NERVA at Jackass Flats, Nevada. This rocket is designed for use only in ground experiments and does not have its equipment arranged as it would be for flight. (Westinghouse Photo)

from their nuclear engines. Besides this, there will be the protection of distance because the nuclear rocket will be on the opposite end of the spacecraft from the crew compartment. If the nuclear rockets need any repairs, the astronauts will have to use remote-control manipulators similar to those used in atomic plants on Earth.

Although it will be used only in space, nuclear rockets will offer a great saving of weight for the interplanetary spacecraft. All fueled and ready to leave parking orbit, the six-man spacecraft powered by three NERVA engines would weigh 1,600,000 pounds. Two of the nuclear engines would be used to start the spacecraft off on its voyage to the planets, and the third would provide power for maneuvering during the flight.

The NERVA reactor operates at 4,940.6° F just a few degrees hotter than a chemically fueled rocket. If it reached any higher heat, the core of the reactor would melt and vaporize. This would be done purposely in the gaseous-core nuclear rocket now under study. Such a rocket could reach temperatures up to 39,140.6° F.

This high temperature gives an added bonus in exhaust velocity by disassociating (separating) the molecules of hydrogen into two atoms, making the exhaust twice as light as the exhaust of a NERVA rocket. As a result, a six-man interplanetary spacecraft powered by a gaseous-core reactor would weigh 800,000 pounds—about half that of a NERVA-powered spacecraft.

Probably the ultimate in rocket power for the interplanetary spacecraft would be to harness the power of the hydrogen bomb in a fusion reactor. So far atomic scientists have been able to produce only brief controlled-fusion reactions. However, in these few seconds temperatures as high as 18,000,000° F were generated. In fact, a temperature of only 9,000,000° F is considered rather low for a controlled fusion reaction.

The first step in controlled-fusion research will be to produce a continued reaction. Next will come fusion reactors for research and electrical power generation. Then, finally, a fusion reactor power rocket will be developed. With such a rocket an interplanetary spacecraft would weigh only 320,000 pounds.

Another way to employ a more efficient rocket would be to use about the same amount of fuel as a chemically fueled rocket but make a quicker trip to the planets and back. One such trip was outlined by Robert G. Ragsdale, a chemical engineer at NASA's Lewis Research Center, in *Astronautics and Aeronautics,* (January, 1972):

> In the early morning light, the space shuttle lifts off the launch pad at Cape Kennedy heading toward a 400-mile orbit. There it releases its payload—a 50,000 pound hydrogen-propellant tank—the last of a series of such deliveries. The hydrogen tank automatically joins a nearby spacecraft. The United States expedition to the planet Mars is ready to begin.
>
> The entire vehicle weighs four and one-half million pounds, three quarters of it hydrogen propellant. The command module, housing five astronauts and their supporting systems, weighs 110,000 lb.—the weight of a fully loaded 737 at take-off. The gaseous-core atomic engine weighs a quarter of a million pounds, and the at-

mospheric reentry vehicle used at mission's end weighs 40,000 lb.

As the rocket reactor comes up to full-rated power of 8,500 MW [Megawatts], it produces 50,000 lb. of thrust which in turn creates a gentle 0.01 g [gravity] force on the crew. As this thrust continues over the next two and one-half days, the Mars rocket spirals out from its initial orbit, finally reaching its terminal velocity of 100,000 fps [feet per second or 68,180 mph] as it enters a trajectory headed for the Red Planet.

Some 30 days and 50-million miles later, a 32-hr. retrofire begins, ending with insertion of the spacecraft in a 200-mi. orbit around Mars. After circling Mars several days for photography and other observations, a 17 hr. thrust maneuver places the ship and crew on a return trajectory. The mission culminates in the atmospheric entry and a final splashdown in the Pacific Ocean.

The total elapsed time between departure from Earth orbit and final splashdown—60 days, the demonstration period of the NASA Skylab program. Thus ends man's first successful voyage to another planet.

Even 68,180 miles per hour is slow compared to the speed a fusion reactor power rocket could reach. In 1953 Dr. Eugen Saenger and his wife, Dr. Irene Saenger-Bredt, pointed out that, like the sun and stars, a fusion reactor would produce a stream of photons (light particles). These photons have a slight amount of pressure as was demonstrated when sunlight pushed the Echo I balloon into a higher orbit in 1960.

The Saengers suggested using a system resembling a

super-powered laser to concentrate the photons from a fusion reactor into a narrow beam with enough force to drive a spaceship. On Earth the atmosphere would absorb most of the energy of this photon rocket—but in space it would have virtually unlimited power and an exhaust velocity of 186,000 miles per *second*.

Given enough acceleration and time, such a rocket could drive a spacecraft to near the speed of light. This would make possible manned flights not only to the inner planets but also to the outer planets of the solar system and eventually even to the nearer stars. Traveling at the speed of light, a spacecraft could reach Venus in 2.76 minutes, Mars in 4.16 minutes, and Mercury in 4.88 minutes.

The catch is that the spacecraft's acceleration must be kept within the limits which a man can stand. Tests have shown that an astronaut lying flat on his back can stand up to 9 g's (nine times earth's gravity) for the short time it takes to go into orbit around Earth. However, to reach speeds approaching the velocity of light, this acceleration would have to continue for fifteen days, which would undoubtedly be too much of a strain on the astronauts. Besides, the spacecraft would be spending far longer getting up speed for the flight than it would making the flight.

A more practical way to use the photon rocket would be to accelerate at 1 g, under which the astronauts have lived practically all their lives, for 10.8 hours. The spacecraft would then head off toward Mars at 2,045,400 miles per hour. Within a day the spacecraft would arrive at Mars and begin a 5.1-hour retrofire to go into orbit around that planet.

About three days would be needed for the landing party to explore a region on Mars. The spacecraft would then make a one-day trip back to Earth. The whole trip would take about six days—two days less than the Apollo 11 moon-landing expedition.

A similar one-day flight could be made to Venus by using the photon rocket. In spite of the fact that a photon rocket would need no help from the sun's gravity, it would still have to start its flight to Venus by heading in the opposite direction from the way Earth revolves around the sun. Otherwise it would add its speed to that of Earth and climb away from the sun toward the orbit of Mars.

To watchers on Earth the takeoff of a photon-powered rocket bound for Venus would be somewhat less spectacular than the launchings by other types of rockets. This is because the spacecraft's photon exhaust, like any beam of light, would be invisible. All that the watchers would see was the spacecraft, which from Earth would look like a bright star, begin to move eastward faster and faster. As it left Earth, the spacecraft would appear fainter and fainter until by the time it reached its top speed of 1,363,600 miles per hour it would be almost out of sight.

Which type of rocket is chosen for the first manned interplanetary spacecraft will naturally depend on what is available at the time construction is started. The NERVA rocket could be ready for flight early in the 1980's according to NASA's latest schedule. The gaseous-core reactor and the photon rocket are not on this schedule. However, the gaseous-core reactor could be ready by the mid 1980's, and the photon rocket could be flying soon after the turn of the century.

3 Getting Ready

Since it is very likely that the first manned interplanetary spacecraft will be powered by flight models of the NERVA rocket, they will have to be assembled in Earth orbit. Early paintings of possible interplanetary spacecraft showed them being constructed in orbit just as a ship is built in a shipyard on earth. However, the Gemini program proved that such a scene is not possible.

In fact, finding ways to work in space without becoming overtired became a major problem for the Gemini astronauts during their space walks. The difficulty is that when an astronaut tries to turn or push on something in space, he tends to turn or drift off in the opposite direction. Proper restraints had to be developed to prevent this.

On November 12, 1966, during his Gemini 12 space walk, astronaut Edwin E. "Buz" Aldrin used a handrail to

GEMINI 12 SPACE WALK: Astronaut Edwin Aldrin retrieves a micrometeoroid detector from the adaptor section of Gemini 12. (NASA Photo)

DEEP SPACE WALK: An artist visualizes how astronaut Al Worden (left) used handrails and footholds to retrieve film cassettes from the service module of Apollo 15 during its return from the moon. (Space Division of North American Rockwell)

move to a work station on the side of the spacecraft. There he practiced a number of tasks such as screwing and unscrewing bolts and moving levers. He used a special screwdriver that absorbed the energy which otherwise would have set him spinning in the opposite direction from his tool. This device served the same purpose as the small rotors of a helicopter which keep the fuselage of the aircraft from spinning in the opposite direction from its big rotors.

While Aldrin worked, he was held in place by a tether similar to a window washer's belt. He also used foot restraints which the astronauts called golden slippers.

These foot restraints worked well, so the golden slippers were also used by astronaut Russell L. Schweickart during his space walk aboard Apollo 9 on March 5, 1969. Astronaut Alfred M. Worden used handrails during his space walk on the Apollo 15 mission on August 5, 1971. For work where no restraints were available an astronaut would need a backpack equipped with steering jets to keep in position.

Astronauts also need restraints for tools and parts. Otherwise they would drift off out of reach. This is what happened to one of astronaut Edward H. White II's outer gloves during his space walk on June 4, 1965, during the Gemini 4 mission. Astronaut Worden used straps to avoid losing the precious canisters which he retrieved from the side of Apollo 15.

Of course, the construction of a spacecraft in orbit would require more than just two or three astronauts. A whole crew, skilled in construction work as well as space walking, would be needed. A space station would also be

SPACE SHIPYARDS: When the day comes for interplanetary space travel, the craft will be assembled in a vast hangar on Earth, like this one conceived by an artist. (General Dynamics/Astronautics)

needed to serve as an orbiting contractor's shack. All this would add needless costs and complications to an already expensive and complicated program.

To avoid these problems, the interplanetary spacecraft would be assembled in modules on Earth. These sections would then be sent into orbit one at a time, then docked together much as the Apollo command module docks with the lunar module.

Dr. Von Braun, speaking to the Senate Aeronautical and Space Sciences Committee on August 5, 1969, described how such a system might work: "We need only two Saturn V's (first two stages only) that we can almost take out of the stable of existing vehicles to provide the earth-to-orbit logistic support for one of these two ships; we need four Saturn V's to support the two ships. One will carry the combined mission module and the MEM, the Mars Exploration Module, and the surface samplers [unmanned probes to precede the manned Mars landing].

"Now assume in the framework of the overall master plan of our manned space flight development . . . that there are two nuclear shuttles in orbit that have supported previously some lunar flights on the basis of reusability, we simply latch onto these and use them as our boosters. They must, of course, first be fueled with liquid hydrogen, but the engine, the tank, and everything else will be in orbit. Should that not be the case, we will need two more Saturn V flights per ship to bring the two boosters up. But in our overall integrated plan which is based on reusability of all this equipment, we can count on these things when we want them."

Besides the nuclear shuttles, diverted from their regular flights between Earth orbit and moon orbit, the mission module for the interplanetary spacecraft would be of the same basic design as those NASA plans to use in manned space stations. The only new design made especially for the interplanetary spacecraft would be the Mars excursion module (MEM).

A similar lander would be carried by the Bikini expedition. Both the Mars and Mercury landers would be based on experience gained from unmanned probes to the surfaces of these planets. They will also draw on the knowledge gained from the lunar module and future moon landers.

If there are any problems in the docking of the sections of the interplanetary spacecraft, a space tug will be put to use. The space tug is a small manned rocket equipped with mechanical hands like those used in an atomic plant. Only if the difficulty is in an area too small for the space tug or its mechanical arms to reach will an astronaut need to don a space suit and go outside to correct it.

Like their spacecraft, the crew for the manned interplanetary flights will have been tested in space. They will be veterans of both Earth orbital and moon flights. Although at least nine years will have elapsed since the last Apollo moon flight, it is still possible that some former Apollo astronauts might be on the first manned interplanetary mission, particularly as commanders.

This would be similar to the experience of Astronaut Alan B. Shepard. Shepard made the United States' first manned spaceflight, a suborbital flight to 116 miles altitude in a Mercury capsule on May 5, 1961. Soon after that he

SPACE TUG: A space shuttle (lower right) has just delivered a space tug (center) to orbit. The tug is maneuvering to dock with a space station module (upper left). A second tug (lower left) adjusts the solar panels on an Orbiting Astronomical Observatory, while a third tug (upper right) boosts an interplanetary probe out of orbit. (NASA Photo)

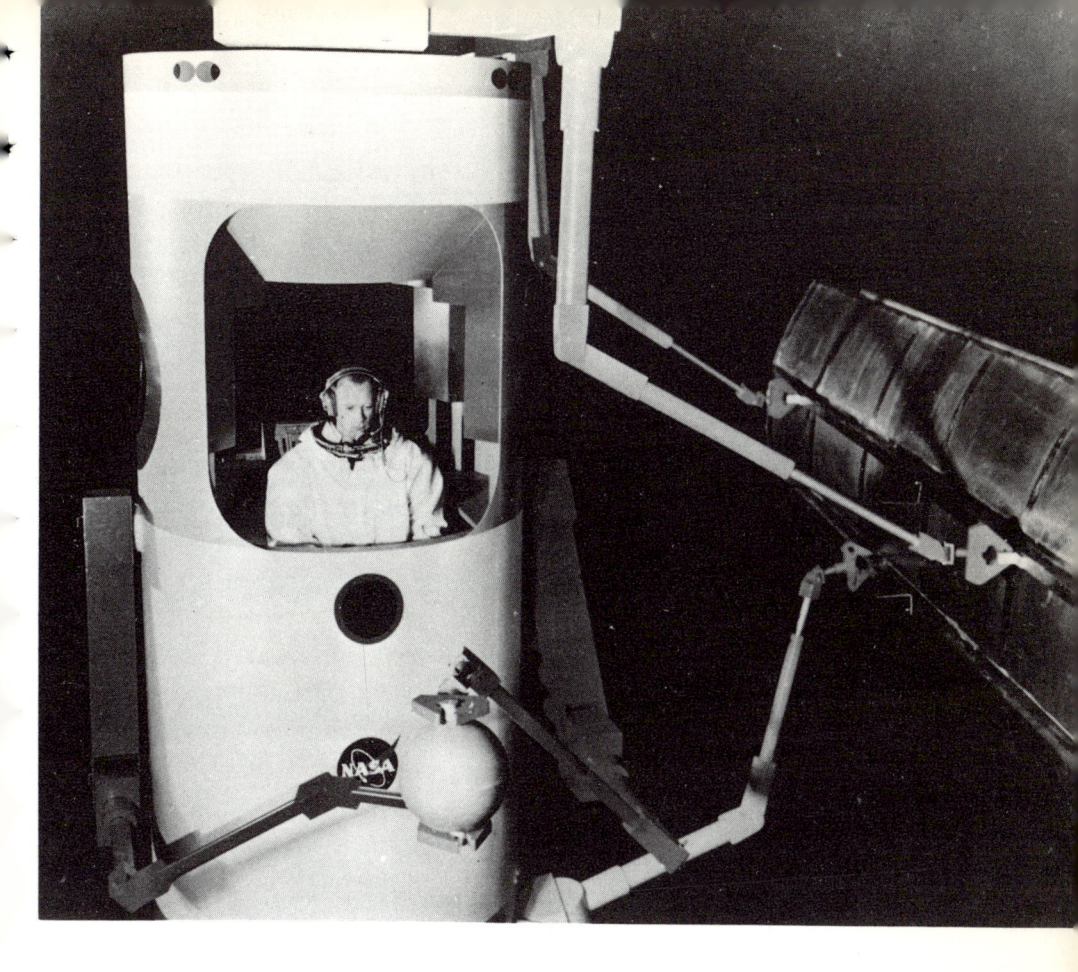

SPACE TAXI: A technician operates a mock-up of a smaller version of the space tug, called a space taxi. Such a craft could maneuver into areas where the larger space tug could not go. Using a space taxi, astronauts would not have to make space walks. (Ling-Temco-Vought, Inc.)

was grounded by an ear ailment. However, he stayed with the manned space program. When surgery corrected his ear trouble, Shepard became commander of the Apollo 14 moon flight which was launched on January 31, 1971.

Besides experience in space, it would help if the interplanetary astronauts had served aboard submarines or underseas habitats. This would give them training in living in a cramped space surrounded by a hostile environment for several months. More specific training for the manned interplanetary flights could be gained by the astronauts' spending several months aboard space stations in earth orbit. Both men and machines would be prepared for the voyages to the planets by such practice.

The crew assignments for interplanetary missions would include both pilot astronauts and scientist astronauts. There would be seven pilot astronauts: a mission commander, three command pilots, and three pilots (one of each for the two interplanetary spacecraft and the lander). The scientist astronauts will be: an astronomer, an exobiologist (a scientist who studies life on other planets), a geologist, a physician, and a meteorologist.

Besides the lander command pilot and pilot, the mission Commander, the Physician, the Exobiologist, and the Geologist would land first on Mars, and on a later flight visit Mercury. Like their predecessors in the Apollo program who trained to explore the moon by exploring areas on Earth which resemble the lunar surface, the members of the landing party would explore areas that resemble the surface of Mars and Mercury. These geological field trips will be made both on Earth and on the moon.

LAUNCHING: With its two booster engines firing, an interplanetary spacecraft begins its journey to Mars. (NASA Photo)

The roving vehicles for exploring Mars and also those for exploring Mercury could be tested on the lunar surface. Our Mariner probes have sent back photographs that show Mars has a rugged terrain much like many areas of the moon. Not nearly so much is known about the surface of Mercury. However, it resembles the cratered highlands of the Moon and Mars.

While Mars and Mercury do have atmospheres, they are too thin and have too little oxygen for internal combustion engines like those used on Earth. This means that any engine that will work on the moon may also be used on Mars and Mercury. These engines would be electric motors powered either by batteries or by fuel cells.

The heat of Mercury could be put to good use to power an engine similar to a miniature steam locomotive. In such an engine a tank, probably painted black to absorb as much heat as possible, would be filled with water. The heat on Mercury would quickly bring the water to a boil. As the steam escaped, it would be used to push pistons, just as it does in a locomotive on Earth. This outer space steam engine could be tested on the moon during the daytime when the temperature reaches 240° F.

Since Mars and Mercury have gravities about one-third that of Earth, the rovers for these planets will have to be weighted to perform under the moon's one-sixth gravity as they would at their destination. However, this would be simpler than suspending two-thirds of the rover's weight with straps as would have to be done on Earth. It would also allow more mobility for the tests.

One area of the moon which would be particularly use-

INTERPLANETARY INSERTION: Having shed its boosters, the interplanetary spacecraft continues under its own power to make the final insertion into a trajectory that will carry it to Mars. (NASA Photo)

ful to the interplanetary astronauts is the region near the crater Aristarchus in the northwestern section of the moon. Near this bright, 29-mile-wide crater, a rill, known as Schroeter's Valley, snakes through the highlands ending in a small plain called the Cobra Head.

This rill and its many branching tributaries look as though they had been created by flowing water—in spite of the fact that the moon is now dry and dusty. Similar regions have been spotted on Mars.

Red flashes of light have also been seen near the Cobra Head and on the rim of the crater Aristarchus by astronomers on Earth. White flashes were seen in this crater by the Apollo 11 astronauts when they passed overhead in moon orbit. This indicates that the region may be volcanic as some areas on Mars appear to be. It is also possible that there may be volcanoes on Mercury.

The interplanetary astronauts will take their spacecraft on shakedown cruises before they actually leave for the planets. These tests will be reminiscent of the Apollo earth-orbiting and moon-orbiting flights that preceded the manned moon landing. However, in the case of the interplanetary spacecraft it will be the ship that is to make the voyage to the planets that receives the tests, not just an exact duplicate.

Probably the first test will be a flight around the moon to test the core of the interplanetary spacecraft without their boosters. Later the booster pairs will be coupled to each of the interplanetary spacecraft and their tanks half filled with fuel for a second circumlunar flight.

For each test flight and for the actual journey to the

planets the interplanetary spacecraft will be refueled by tanker rockets launched from Earth. The same techniques perfected by the Air Force for midair refueling will work equally well for refueling in orbit.

Now, with all the training and testing completed and with fuel tanks full, the interplanetary expedition will finally be ready to go. The two booster rockets on both spacecraft will fire simultaneously. Once the interplanetary spacecraft are off on their way to their destination the boosters will separate and loop back to Earth—already a quarter of a million miles distant.

4 Convoy to Mars

The serious problem that must be solved before an interplanetary flight is whether people can survive months of weightlessness. A number of tests have indicated that possibly people cannot.

Even on short flights of a week or two astronauts have shown a loss of calcium balance and other slowly accumulating ailments. Over several months such problems might develop into a serious, possibly even fatal disability.

One of the major studies of NASA's Skylab project is the long-term effects of weightlessness. Yet the longest flights aboard Skylab were scheduled to last barely two months. To make certain that weightlessness is no barrier to interplanetary flights, these long voyages must be simulated in space stations orbiting Earth.

If weightlessness over long periods is indeed found to

be a hazard, then some form of artificial gravity will be needed. Perhaps only a few minutes or hours of gravity will suffice. In this case each interplanetary spacecraft will carry a small centrifuge. This device resembles a souped-up carnival ride. The astronaut will enter a car either at the end of a long boom or riding on a circular track. The car will then spin faster and faster. The force of this rotation will cause the astronaut to be pressed against the outside wall of the car—just as gravity causes us to be pressed against the floor or the ground on Earth.

If such short periods of artificial gravity are found not to be enough, the entire mission module will have to be rotated to provide the same type of artificial gravity. One problem with this second method is that the force is less near the center of the craft where the spin is slower. This means that if the ship were too small, the astronauts' heads would feel lighter than their feet. To solve this problem, the decks where the crew will spend most of their time should be about 100 feet from the center of rotation.

NASA planners have proposed that once they are on their way to the planets, the two interplanetary spacecraft be docked nose to nose and rotated. This would make it easy for the astronauts to go from ship to ship during the flight, and the lower decks of each mission module would be the proper distance apart. However, the highest artificial gravity would be at the reactor ends of the spacecraft where it is not needed.

Docking the ships rocket engine to rocket engine would solve this problem, but then the astronauts would have to pass the radioactive reactors when they went from ship to ship.

Leaving the two spacecraft undocked and spinning each one separately would give both the reactor and the living quarter the maximum amount of artificial gravity. However, this would mean that the astronauts would have to travel through space to transfer from one ship to another.

Besides, whatever way is used to rotate an entire spacecraft it will make navigation and keeping in radio contact with Earth difficult. Imagine trying to make a sighting on a star when the whole universe appears to be spinning. About all you would get is dizzy.

Rotating an entire ship would also mean wasting steering jet fuel to turn parts that did not really need to rotate. Then whenever the nuclear rocket had to be used for a course correction or to go into orbit around a planet, the rotation would have to be stopped and then started again after the maneuver—all of which would use still more fuel.

A better way would be to rotate only the living quarters. For this, at least two sections of the mission module would extend out long booms to provide proper balance. Such a shape is too ungainly for launch from Earth because of air resistance and the high acceleration of the launching rocket. In space, however, they would be no problem, and in fact, they would be nothing unusual. Like other spacecraft before it, the mission module will be sent into Earth orbit folded and will then unfold either like a telescope or an umbrella. Steering jets will then start the mission module turning.

The rotating mission module will be connected to the rest of the ship by an axle so that the ship proper would remain stationary. A similar device was used on NASA's orbiting solar observatories (OSO), the first of which was launched on March 7, 1962. Part of the OSO was kept continually pointed toward the sun while another part spun, providing stability like a gyroscope. The rotating mission module would provide the same stabilizing effect for the interplanetary spacecraft.

An astronaut will enter the rotating mission module through a docking collar and airlock at the front of the axle. He will then crawl through a hatch, feet first, into the hub of the mission module. Stepping onto the slowly moving floor will be as easy as stepping onto an escalator. The only way the astronaut will notice the rotation at this point will be if he looks up and sees that he is slowly moving away from the hatch through which he just came. If he waits at least twenty-four seconds, he will pass underneath the hatch again.

From the hub he can either take an elevator or walk down a spiral staircase to the lower decks. There would not be room even in a large interplanetary spacecraft for a straight staircase, so an elevator will be needed to handle items which cannot be negotiated around the winding stairs. The staircase will start down at a steep angle, then gradually flatten out to a more gentle slope as the gravity increases.

Even at the bottom of the stairs there will probably not be a full Earth gravity. This would require a too heavy structure to withstand the rapid rotation of once every eight seconds or 7.5 revolutions per minute. It would be better if just enough artificial gravity were provided to keep the astronauts from suffering the ill effects of weightlessness. Another possibility is to copy the one-third gravity of Mars

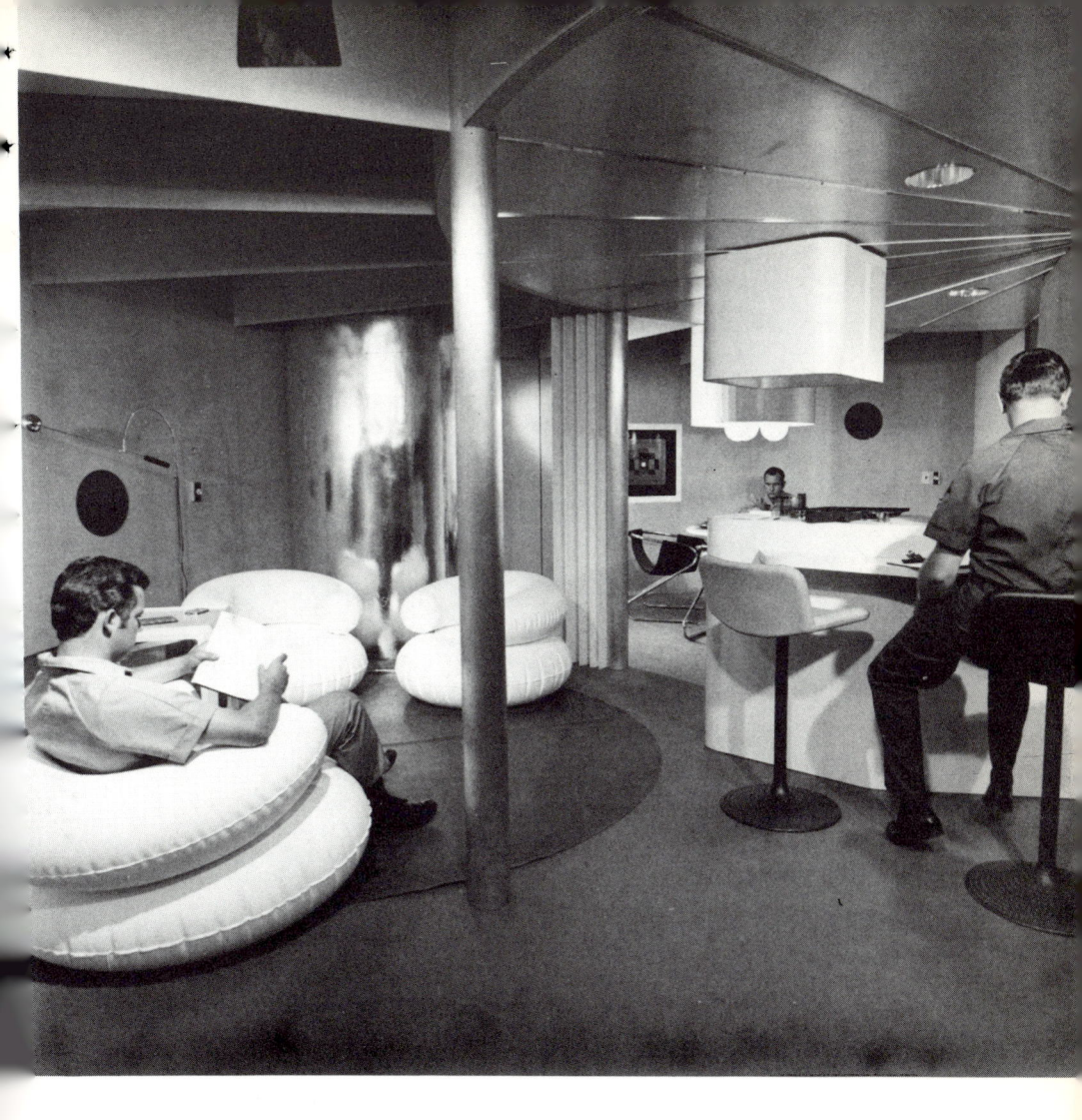

LIVING QUARTERS: How the wardroom of an interplanetary spacecraft with artificial gravity might look. The furniture is extremely light to save weight. Yet, as the photo shows, it can support a man even under the full gravity of Earth. (Grumman Aircraft Corp.)

and Mercury so that when the astronauts arrive, they will be used to working under its pull.

Besides preventing any ill effects from weightlessness, artificial gravity would be a convenience and economy for the interplanetary expedition. The astronauts could drink from glasses instead of squeezing the liquid from plastic bags. In the spacecraft's laboratories they could also use off-the-shelf equipment from Earth, such as beakers and scales. This would be much less expensive than using equipment made especially for space.

Regardless of whether or not the spacecraft has artificial gravity, the astronauts will still have to exercise to keep fit for the work that will come when the landing is made. The difference would be in the types of exercise performed. On a weightless spacecraft the crew would work out on exercycles, bungee cords, and spring-tension devices. With artificial gravity they could jog, run up and down the stairs, and practice gymnastics.

Some of the food eaten by the astronauts might be grown aboard the interplanetary spacecraft if all the wastes were recycled in a closed ecology. This is the way nature does on our giant spacecraft, Earth—when it has a chance.

In 1969 NASA's Langley Research Center in Virginia began tests of a space station simulator with a life-support system that could recycle air and water. Engineers are investigating ways of adding the third life-support element—food—to the recycling system, making a completely closed ecology.

At the opposite extreme from a closed ecology is an open life-support system in which everything is used once and

LIFE IN WEIGHTLESSNESS: Astronauts aboard a weightless spacecraft use a variety of devices to overcome the inconveniences of zero gravity. A flow of air keeps stray droplets of water from drifting out of the shower stall and washbasin. The astronaut at left will use a netting to keep himself from floating out of bed while he sleeps. (Grumman Aircraft Corp.)

simply ejected from the spacecraft. The amount of equipment and supplies needed for an open life-support system would weigh three times as much as one that only recycled oxygen and water. This added weight might not just go along for the ride. Until it was needed, it could serve as a radiation shield.

Extra shielding would have to be carried if a closed ecology were used. The added weight of this shielding would make the total weight of the mission module 72,000 pounds. This is just 16,000 pounds less than one with an open life-support system, which would weigh 88,000 pounds.

Still, one of the cardinal rules of spaceflight is: Save as much weight as possible. Besides, even if the spacecraft could carry an extra 8 tons without any difficulty, this weight allowance might better be used for some more useful equipment.

A closed ecology has more to offer than just weight savings. The wastes ejected from the open system would not fall behind the spacecraft but would remain alongside until the ship changed course. In the meantime the spacecraft would have become surrounded by a cloud of waste.

This waste cloud would make it difficult for the navigator or the automatic guidance system to take the sightings necessary to line up the craft for maneuver. He might mistake the sunlight reflected off a discarded can for the star he was to make a sighting on.

Similarly, John Glenn thought for a moment, when he first saw them, that the frost flakes shaken from the walls of his Mercury capsule were a new star field.

An oxygen-recycling system that would work on the interplanetary spacecraft has already been used in NASA's space station simulator. The operation of this system was described in the NASA Facts publication on *Living in Space* (April, 1969):

> . . . air first passes through fiber-glass filters which remove visible-size particles. The air then flows through charcoal filters, which remove odors and certain unwanted gases.
>
> Beyond the filter, air is passed through a device called a catalytic burner which changes any trace quantities of toxic gases into harmless compounds. Then all the air flows through the cabin heat exchanger which cools the air to a temperature which maintains the cabin at a comfortable range. In passing through this unit, most of the moisture contained in the air changes to tiny droplets of water which are siphoned off into the water storage tanks for later purification and reuse.

NASA's system next uses mechanical means to remove the carbon dioxide from the air. The interplanetary rocket, however, would probably use green plants instead. The plants take in carbon dioxide and water, which, with the energy from sunlight, they separate into oxygen and hydrocarbons through photosynthesis. The oxygen is returned to the air, and the hydrocarbons form part of the plant's tissue. This tissue could provide at least part of the food for the astronauts.

The plant most often suggested for use in such a system is *Chlorella,* a form of alga. It is alga that forms the green scum on stagnant water. These green water plants are already used as a very nutritious food in the Orient. It can be made very tasty, but the astronauts will probably also want some other plants for variety.

Of course, green plants will have to be tested in space before the interplanetary flight. The effects of varying amounts of sunlight, and other solar radiation, which the plants will receive from the orbit of Mercury out to the orbit of Mars must be tested. If this radiation proves harmful to the plants, they will have to be grown under artificial light.

How weightlessness affects the plants must also be learned. For instance, would alga float on the surface of the water if it were weightless? And would a seed be able to send its leaves up and its roots down if there were no gravity to tell it which way was which?

This brings up another problem: What effect would spaceflight have on the circadian rhythms of the plants and those of the astronauts as well? These are the biological clocks that regulate the behavior of all living things, including man. Experiments have shown that these rhythms continue even when an organism is shielded from all the normal signs of the passage of time. This raises the question: Are they governed by some outside force which cannot be screened on Earth—but which might not operate the same way in space? Or are these rhythms a built-in part of the organism independent of its surroundings?

If all the oxygen used by the astronauts were recycled, 120 pounds of oxygen would last the spacecraft's crew of six for their entire lifetime—if there were no leakage. No vessel can be made completely leakproof, especially since

ROTATING SPACECRAFT: This depicts an Apollo spacecraft docking at the hub of a "Paddle Wheel" space station which is manned by from twelve to twenty-four people and rotates to provide artificial gravity. (NASA Photo)

the astronauts will be climbing in and out to explore the planets and possibly to make repairs. This means that 150 extra pounds of air will be needed for each ninety days of flight.

Of course, each spacecraft will carry an additional 120 pounds of oxygen just in case the entire twelve-man crew has to double up in one ship. Both ships would also have backup life-support systems.

The air aboard the interplanetary spacecraft will not be pure oxygen, as it was on the Apollo moon flights. Doctors have found that pure oxygen would be harmful to astronauts even for the comparatively short mission of the Skylab. This is why NASA switched to a two-gas atmosphere of 69 percent oxygen and 31 percent nitrogen at about 5 pounds per square inch for the Skylab project.

A two-gas atmosphere does not necessarily have to be a miniature copy of Earth's air. Other spacecraft designs have proposed a helium and oxygen combination. Among these was the Air Force's two-manned version of the Skylab, the manned orbital laboratories (MOL). Because of lack of funds, the MOL was canceled after its first unmanned flights.

Helium has several advantages over the nitrogen which makes up most of Earth's atmosphere. For one thing, helium does not cause the bends or aeroembolism as nitrogen does when the pressure drops too swiftly. In this ailment the nitrogen dissolved in the bloodstream forms bubbles as the pressure drops rapidly. This causes severe pain and may cause death.

For this reason, helium rather than nitrogen is often used

in the high-pressure atmospheres of underseas dwellings. This use of helium causes the divers' voices to become high and squeaky. However, distortions are also produced in a high-pressure nitrogen-oxygen atmosphere. This indicates that there should not be too great a problem with distortion in the low-pressure atmosphere of a spacecraft.

Rapid drops in pressure are not as great a problem for astronauts as they are to deep-sea divers. A diver must undergo decompression in order to return to the surface from the depths. This drop in pressure must be made gradually in order to avoid the bends. By contrast, an astronaut goes from a low-pressure atmosphere to a higher-pressure atmosphere when he emerges from his spacecraft on Earth.

The only time an astronaut would be in danger of sudden decompression would be if a meteoroid punctured his spacecraft. Space probes have reported increasing numbers of meteoroids as they near Mars. In spite of this, it is unlikely that at any time during its entire spaceflight the interplanetary spacecraft would encounter a meteoroid large enough to penetrate its hull.

Still, to be on the safe side the spacecraft will have a double hull called a meteoroid bumper. Inside these double hulls the spacecraft will be divided into a number of airtight sections linked by airlocks. Thus, if one chamber is punctured, the astronauts can escape to the neighboring compartments, then return in space suits to repair the damage. Spare tanks of air would be carried to replace the atmosphere lost during this accident.

Even if a small meteoroid did puncture both hulls of the spacecraft, this would not cause a sudden decompression any more than a nail hole causes a blowout in a tire. What would happen is that a leak detector would sound an alarm and flash a light on the spacecraft's control panel. The air-circulation system would automatically compensate for the drain on the air supply while the astronauts found the leak and plugged it.

They would probably first release a small cloud of smoke from an aerosol can. The smoke will flow with the air escaping through the hole, revealing the puncture's location to the astronauts. They would then plug the hole with a rubber disk, resembling a sink stopper, until a permanent repair can be made.

A sudden decompression would occur only if a meteoroid nearly a foot or more wide hit the spacecraft. Such an event would require no alarms. The meteoroid would announce itself with a loud bang as it crashed through the hull of the spacecraft and embedded itself in the opposite bulkhead. Immediately all the air in the damaged compartment would rush out of the gaping hole, drawing any loose objects with it. Automatic pressure gauges would close air vents to the compartment, preventing the rest of the spacecraft's air from escaping.

Any unfortunate astronauts caught in this compartment would not be in quite such a predicament as is sometimes expected. As Arthur C. Clarke says in *The Exploration of Space*:

> It has often been suggested that the crew of a punctured spaceship would be killed instantly and their bodies perhaps ruptured by the expansion of internal gases when

Before launch.

4 hours and 40 minutes of weightlessness.

12 hours and 29 minutes of weightlessness.

17 hours and 40 minutes of weightlessness.

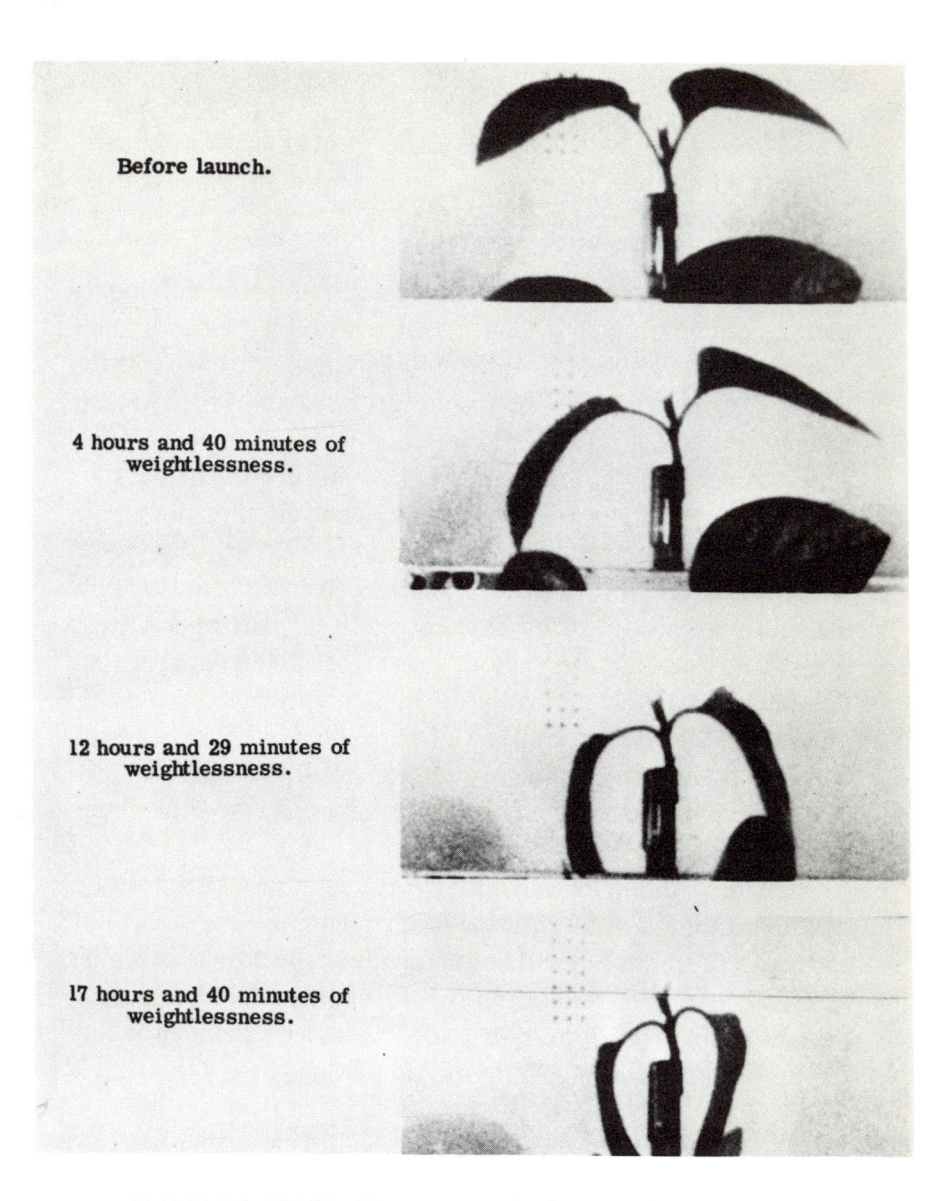

PLANT IN SPACE: This series of photographs shows the effects of weightlessness on a pepper plant carried by Biosatellite 2 during its September 7–9, 1967, flight. (NASA Photo)

the pressure was released. This is not the case. Numerous tests have now been made of healthy human subjects and it has been found that a pressure drop of seven and a half pounds per square inch, occurring in less than half a second can be tolerated.

The astronauts would have twelve seconds to reach safety before unconsciousness and death overtook them. If their escape was successful, they will, thanks to the oxygen-helium atmosphere of their spacecraft, suffer no ill effects except perhaps a severe emotional shock.

Fortunately it is unlikely that a spacecraft will ever be hit by a foot-wide meteorite. They are even rare on Earth.

A more likely, although still remote, threat to the spacecraft is the possibility of fire. The specter of a catastrophic fire has haunted NASA ever since three astronauts were killed in a flash fire aboard an Apollo spacecraft on January 27, 1967. Since that time everything that could be made out of fireproof materials has been. Objects which cannot be fireproofed are kept in fireproof lockers. All these precautions will be followed aboard the interplanetary spacecraft.

If a fire should break out in spite of these precautions, the astronauts could either douse it with fire extinguishers or seal off the compartment and allow the fire to smother itself. The smoke remaining from this fire could be cleared by canisters of lithium hydroxide, the same chemical which is used to remove carbon dioxide aboard Apollo spacecraft.

The oxygen used up by the fire would be replaced from the spacecraft's emergency tanks.

Little, if any, extra water will be needed to handle either fires or loss through meteoroid punctures. This is due to the fact that the human body actually produces about a pint more water per day than it takes in. The extra water comes from part of the oxygen inhaled combining with hydrogen in the man's food.

Besides the water already wrung out of the air by the dehumidifiers in the air-circulation system, more will be collected from the astronauts' urine and wash water. This waste water will be collected in tanks until there is enough for recycling. Meanwhile, it will be purified and deodorized with chlorine and other chemicals.

If artificial gravity is used, the waste water could serve as a counterweight to balance the movements of the crew. When an astronaut moved from one side of the mission module to the other, he would cause a weight shift which would cause the mission module to wobble. Sensitive gauges would detect this wobble and pump water from one end of the mission module to the other, counteracting the wobble and relieving the strain on the spacecraft's structure.

To begin the recycling process, warm dry air will be blown over the waste water, causing it to evaporate. If the spacecraft is weightless, a wick will be needed for this evaporation. The evaporated water is then sent through a charcoal filter and condensed for reuse. Some of this water would be cooled for drinking, and the rest would be left hot for washing and cooking.

NASA has suggested that the astronauts might be squeamish about using water reclaimed from their urine. However, this situation is no worse than the case of most municipal water systems on Earth which purify water from streams used to carry off the wastes from farms and other communities upstream.

Also in the manner of Earth part of the astronauts' feces might be used as fertilizer for the plants in the spacecraft's greenhouse. Some of the feces could also be filtered through redwood fibers. The remaining protein wastes would then be fed to scavenger fish which would be added to the astronauts' diet. Since scavenger fish include such things as snails and lobsters, the crew would have some real gourmet meals. Of course the fish will have to be tested in the environment of space as were the plants.

Even the fanciest fare begins to pall after a long time as a steady diet. Therefore, some conventional freeze dried and condensed food may be included for variety. Powdered flavorings will also be needed for the astronauts' drinks. Carrying along plants that produce these flavors would be impractical since most of them are rather large and others bear only one crop a year.

Some planners have suggested that the astronauts not needed for the flight to the planets should go into hibernation until they reach their destination. In this way they would avoid the boredom of a long flight and cause less strain on the life-support systems.

Many animals pass the lean months of winter in hibernation. However, the mechanism which induces this suspended animation and brings the animals out of it in the spring is not known. This mechanism would have to be found and some way developed to adapt it to human beings before it could be applied to spaceflight.

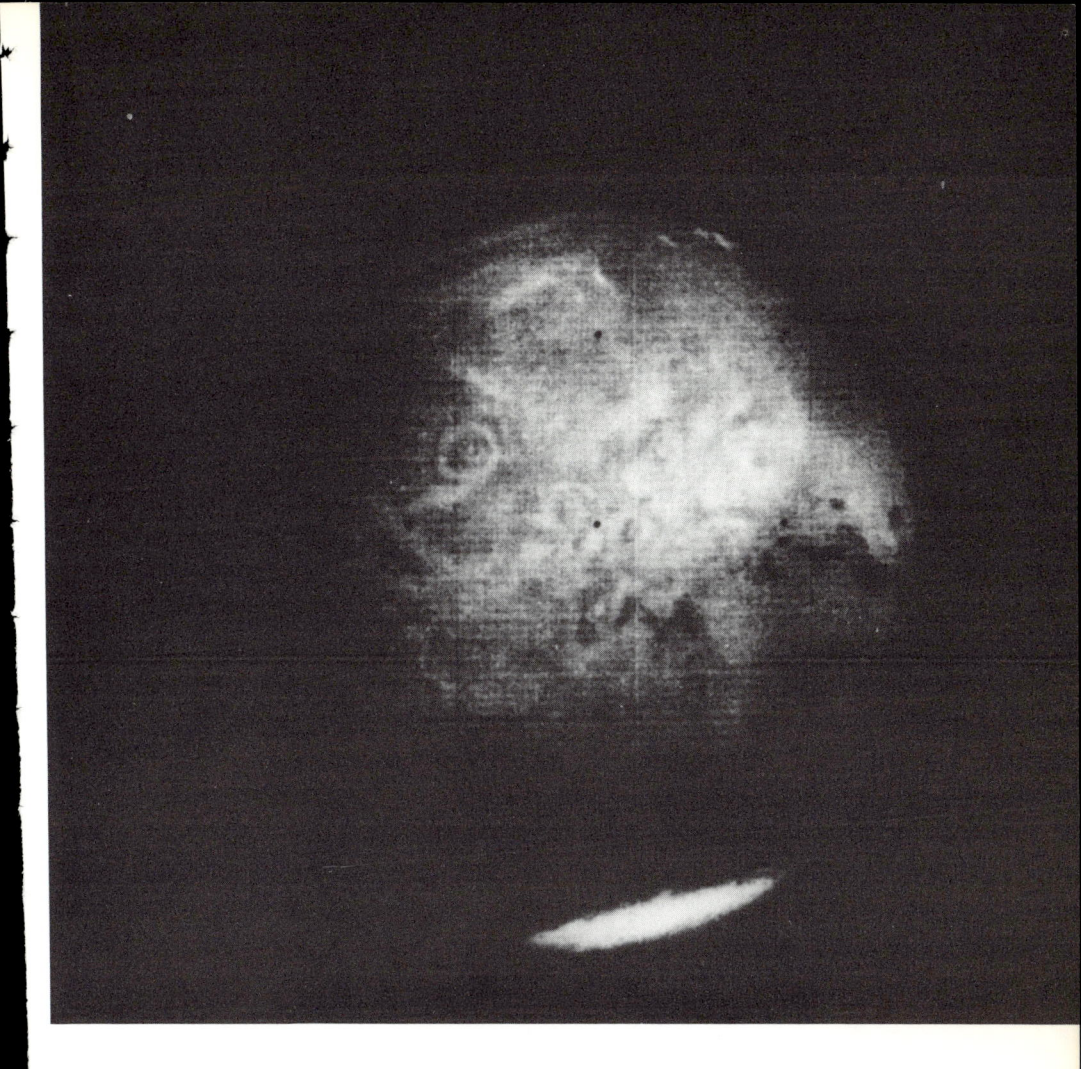

APPROACHING MARS: The first astronauts to visit Mars will have a view similar to this just before they go into orbit around Mars. This photo was taken by Mariner 7 on August 4, 1969, at 293,200 miles from the planet. (NASA Photo)

Once the secret of hibernation was discovered, it is possible that the equipment needed to sustain this state on a comparatively short flight to the inner planets might use more space and weight than the life-support system needed for normal life especially with a closed ecology system. On longer flights to planets beyond Mars and particularly those to other stars, hibernation may be needed.

As for boredom, flights to and from our neighboring planets will be anything but dull. The pilot astronauts will be occupied with standing watch over the spacecrafts' systems. On moon flights and Earth orbital missions this job is performed by mission control. The flight controllers would also keep a close eye on interplanetary flights. However, because of the time it takes light to cross the void between planets, the flight controllers would not be able to respond quickly enough in an emergency.

During their journey to Mars or Mercury the astronauts and the meteorologist will be busy preparing their landing craft and other equipment needed for the trip to the planet's surface. On the return flight they will be evaluating the data collected during that expedition.

Throughout the flight the astronomer will be studying the stars and planets. He will be seeing these objects as no other man has ever seen them.

Besides treating any ills or injuries that arise during the flight, the physician will be monitoring the effects of spaceflight on the astronauts.

5 Exploring Mars

With all their activity the astronauts will have only a few moments to notice the Earth shrinking behind them and their destination planet growing larger. Soon this alien planet will be changed from a tiny star into a huge globe dominating the sky. The time will then have arrived to begin the braking maneuver and go into orbit around the planet.

The astronauts will assemble in the control room of the two ships to begin the deceleration. The astronauts will carefully run through a checklist of their equipment, position the spacecraft, and then restart the nuclear rockets. If the deceleration is less than the force of the artificial gravity, it will not affect the equipment in the rotating module. Otherwise, any loose objects will have to be stowed away before the rockets fire to avoid having objects clatter to the back of the cabin.

The first planet visited by astronauts will most likely be Mars. Like their predecessors in the Apollo moon program, the astronauts will now give the folks back home on Earth a description of the alien landscape beneath the spacecraft.

In an article in *National Geographic* (August, 1970) Kenneth F. Weaver described the view from orbit above Mars:

> Craters dominate the landscape. We can see no mountain chains, no bodies of water, no canals. The atmosphere seems clear almost to the horizon, where a narrow rim of bluish haze, with an occasional bright patch, gives way quickly to the blackness of space.
>
> And out in that blackness, 130,000,000 miles away, shines a diminished sun, two-thirds its remembered size. Only half as much solar energy is falling on Mars as on Earth.

Besides the craters, there are several large volcanoes on the mottled burned ocher and grayish red globe of Mars. The volcanoes are quiet now, but the interplanetary astronauts could be treated to the spectacle of an un-Earthly eruption.

Of greatest interest to the astronauts will be the puzzling features they have come to investigate. There are two polar caps made up of frozen carbon dioxide and ice frost. One cap will probably appear near its full extent, while the other will have almost, if not completely, disappeared in the Martian summer.

WOLF TRAP

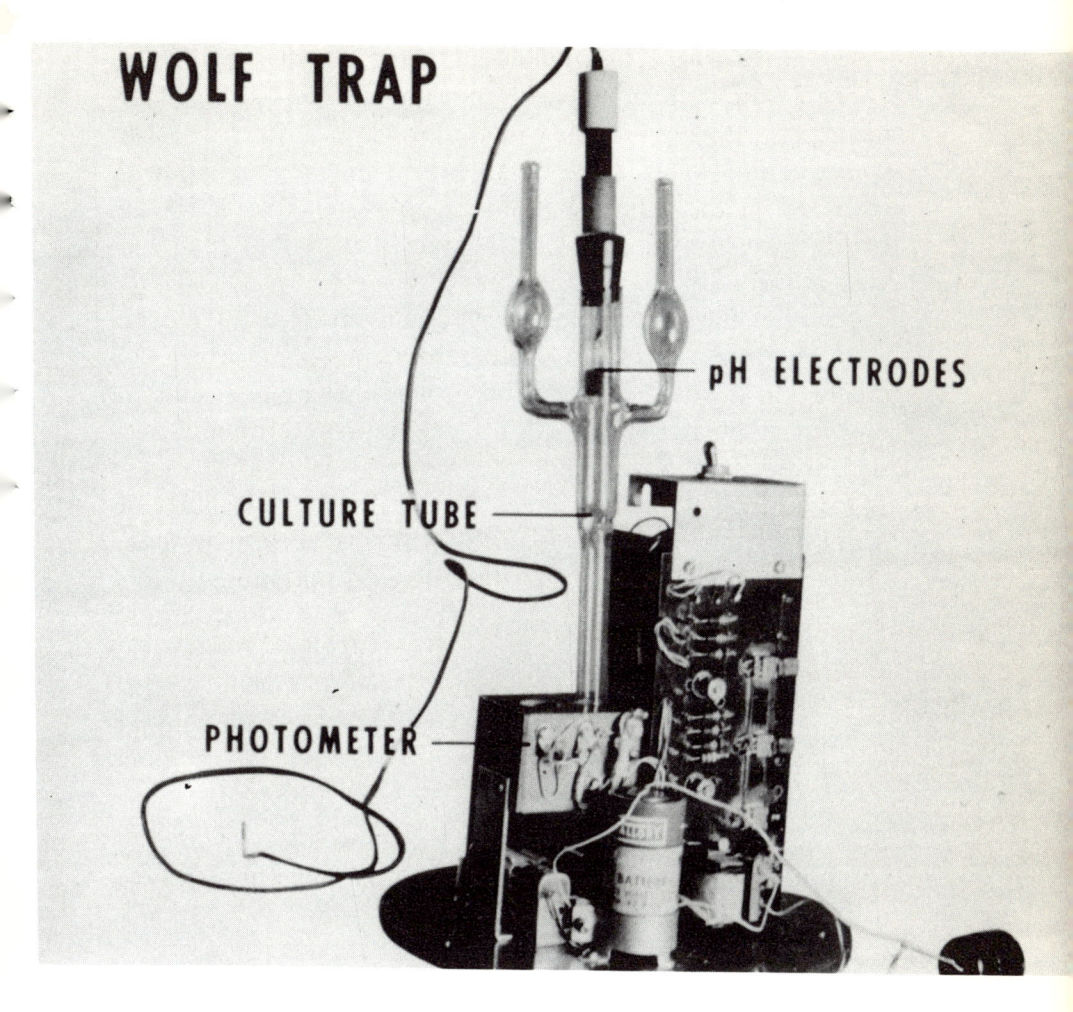

pH ELECTRODES

CULTURE TUBE

PHOTOMETER

WOLF TRAP: This device, designed by Wolf Vishniac of the University of Rochester, could be used by astronauts or an unmanned probe to detect life on other planets. After landing, it sucks up samples of a planet's soil and air, then injects them into a bacteria culture. If the sample contains living organisms, their growth will cause the clear broth to cloud. (NASA Photo)

Equatorward of the polar cap, dark blotches will have appeared in that hemisphere of Mars, while in the other hemisphere the markings will be growing lighter. It is as if vegetation were springing to life in one region while it withered in the other. Yet no green plants like those on Earth have been detected on Mars. In fact, that planet is very inhospitable to Earthly life.

Another puzzle are the riverlike canyons that have been seen on Mars—a planet with hardly enough moisture to create a heavy dew. Perhaps water was once more abundant on Mars. The astronauts will be seeking to determine where such water may have gone.

In contrast with the rugged terrain that covers parts of Mars, there are also vast featureless plains. Probably these are covered by fine, shifting dust. It was undoubtedly this dust which caused the huge planetwide dust storm which frustrated scientists' efforts to photograph Mars for several weeks after Mariner 9 went into orbit on November 14, 1971. It is hoped that the manned expedition will find better weather when they arrive.

From the reports of earlier unmanned probes and their own observations the astronauts will now select a landing site somewhere within reach of as many interesting features as possible. They will then plot a trajectory to carry a landing craft to this spot.

Before the manned landing an unmanned probe will be sent down to examine this site. It will collect samples of the Martian soil and air and return these to the orbiting spacecraft. Examination of these samples will tell the astronauts what to expect when they make their landing.

MARS LANDING VEHICLE: Having shed its heat shield, a MEM descends to the Martian surface under a broad parachute. Its rocket engine will be used to cushion the final landing. (General Dynamics/Astronautics)

After undocking from the interplanetary spacecraft, the cone-shaped Mars excursion module will enter the Martian atmosphere broad end first. Like an Apollo spacecraft re-entering Earth's atmosphere, the MEM will be slowed by air drag. When the spacecraft has dropped to below the speed of sound, the heat shield will be jettisoned. Rockets will then be used for the final descent. The astronauts will carefully steer the spacecraft to a touchdown on a smooth and not too dusty landing site.

Now comes that historic moment when man first sets foot on Mars. Undoubtedly the mission commander will have spent much of his spare time on the flight from Earth thinking of appropriate remarks for this moment. These remarks and the television pictures of the first Mars walk will reach Earth in about 4.16 minutes traveling at the speed of light.

If the pictures are in color, the viewers will see space-suited figures moving about a white spacecraft standing on an ocher-colored desert. The sky overhead is deep purple with the brighter stars shining even in the daytime. The astronauts will point out one starlike object of particular interest to themselves and to the viewers: the bright bluish-white Earth shining near the sun just above the reddish hills on the eastern horizon. This horizon is about twice as close as that on Earth since Mars is about half the size of our planet.

The Martian atmosphere is only about as thick as Earth's air is at 20 miles altitude. This makes it much too thin for an astronaut to survive without a pressure suit. Besides, the Martian air is mostly carbon dioxide, so it cannot even

MARS MOON PROBE: An unmanned probe detached from one of the interplanetary spacecraft approaches one of Mars' small moons. (General Dynamics/Astronautics)

be compressed for breathing as airliners do Earth's upper air.

Astronauts on Mars will have what will be a rare luxury for space explorers: the opportunity to work in sunlight and sleep at night. This is because the days on Mars are twenty-four hours and thirty-seven minutes long—just a little longer than the length of those the astronauts grew up under on Earth.

At midday on Mars' equator, where the landing will probably be made, the astronaut will find the temperature a warm 80° F. If he ventures out at night, however, the astronaut will need an extra coat over his space suit, for then the temperature drops to $-50°$ F.

The heat needed in the MEM during these frigid nights, as well as the electrical equipment aboard the MEM, will probably receive power from a nuclear isotope-powered generator. Like the NERVA rocket engine, the nuclear isotope-powered generator uses the energy of a nuclear reaction to heat a working fluid. This fluid then turns a turbine which produces the electricity. The working fluid could be passed through a heat exchanger to boil water. providing steam heat for the MEM. After this, the working fluid would be cooled in a radiator outside the spacecraft and returned to the generator for reuse.

The spent steam from the heaters will be allowed to condense and be returned to the heat exchanger for reuse. This nuclear generator will be similar to those used to power the experiments left on the moon by the Apollo astronauts.

When the astronaut looks into Mars' night sky, he will see the familiar stars and constellations he saw on Earth.

MARS INITIAL LANDING: Members of the landing party collect samples of the Martian surface in this artist's concept. (NASA Photo)

They will shine with a much brighter and steadier light than they do even in the clear desert air on Earth. The principle difference will be that the whole sky will seem to have shifted about 30° to the south-southwest. This is due to Mars' north pole pointing at a spot midway between the stars Deneb and Zeta Cephei instead of at Polaris, Earth's polestar.

There will be no huge moon to illuminate the Martian night—just two tiny moons: Phobos, which is about 15.5 by 13 miles, and Deimos, which is about 8 by 7 miles. Deimos will appear almost stationary in the sky as it takes 1.26 days to circle Mars in an orbit at 14,600-mile altitude. The speedier Phobos, just 5,830 miles above Mars, circles that planet about three times a day.

The astronaut will also see the reassuring sight of two bright points of light in the Martian night sky, revealing the presence of the interplanetary spacecraft waiting for the return flight.

The astronauts left aboard the interplanetary craft will not be just sitting around waiting, however. They will be busy mapping Mars and studying its moons. Unmanned probes will be sent to both Deimos and Phobos. If the expedition has a space tug along, manned visits could be made to these two crater-pocked moons which resemble giant stone Irish potatoes.

A crucial task will be performed by the expedition's meteorologist. It will be his task to keep an eye on the Martian weather and give warning if any large dust storms develop. If this happens, the astronauts on Mars will have to cut short their activities and head back to orbit.

HOMEWARD BOUND: Leaving the ascent stage of the MEM behind, an interplanetary rocket heads back to Earth. (NASA Photo)

Another hazard to the astronauts may come from living organisms on Mars. The danger will probably not come from attacks by the bug-eyed monsters that often threaten comic-strip spacemen but from microorganisms. These Martian germs could give the astronauts some unknown disease.

In spite of the harsh conditions on Mars, it is still possible that life could survive there. Some Earthly bacteria have been able to live in simulated Martian environments. Thus life on Mars could have evolved when conditions there were more favorable and might then have adapted to the changing conditions. It is also possible that Martian life may be based on a different chemical formula from Earthly life.

To prevent any Martian germs from getting into the MEM, the astronauts will follow precautions like those taken by astronauts on the first three Apollo moon explorations. After each exploration the astronauts will carefully brush off dust particles. Any particles that do not brush off can be vacuumed off. For more safety the astronauts can hang their space suits in airtight closets in the airlock. This will keep them from tracking any dust into the cabin. Filters will remove any dust that gets into the air.

If there are any living organisms on Mars, they won't all be left behind. Some will be brought back for study. The exobiologist will seal these samples in study cases that can come safely through even a crash landing. These cases will be connected to their own life-support system to provide the organisms with an environment like that of Mars.

While the exobiologist is collecting specimens of Martian life, or at least those that show its possibility, the geologist will be gathering samples of the Mars rocks and dust. Like the living organisms, these samples will be sealed in sturdy airtight cases.

A clue to where Mars' water went may be found in the Martian dust. Most astronomers believe that Mars gets its reddish color from iron rust. However, Dr. William T. Plummer and Robert K. Carson, of the University of Massachusetts, report that the spectrum of Mars looks like that of carbon suboxide. This substance turns orange or reddish brown when bombarded with ultraviolet radiation which penetrates the thin Martian atmosphere. However, carbon suboxide is a relatively rare substance on Earth.

If there is abundant carbon suboxide on Mars, the astronauts will know it the moment they take off their space helmets after returning to the airlock. This substance has the odor of old sweat socks.

It is also possible that some of the water on Mars may be found frozen beneath the surface. Core samples will be drilled out to check on this and other substances that may lie beneath the surface of Mars.

After carefully examining the area surrounding the landing site, the astronauts will take field trips to other interesting locations nearby. Unless the Mars rover has an enclosed cabin, these expeditions will have to get back to the MEM before sunset—even though their space suits would keep the astronauts warm. Mars is no place to camp out under the stars!

Two rovers will also be needed if overnight trips are to

be made. Otherwise, the ventures will have to be kept short enough for the astronauts to walk back if the rover breaks down. With two rovers three or four of the astronauts could take one on a field trip. If there is any trouble, the astronauts on the field trip will radio those in the orbiting interplanetary spacecraft, who will relay the message to the astronauts in the MEM. Two of these astronauts will then set out on a rescue mission in the spare rover.

Before returning to the interplanetary spacecraft, the landing party will set up automatic equipment to continue the investigation of Mars. This equipment would include instruments to measure: solar radiation received by Mars; changes in the composition of the air from dust storms, etc.; the changing air pressure and humidity on Mars; a seismograph to detect Marsquakes; and a life detector.

Also left behind will be the Mars rovers, the astronauts' dusty overboots, and the television camera set up right after the landing. If this camera is still working, television viewers on Earth will get to watch the takeoff from Mars. At the moment of launch the top portion of the MEM will lift off and climb rapidly out of sight trailing a long white plume of flame. This is the ascent stage of the MEM carrying astronauts back to the waiting interplanetary spacecraft.

When the ascent stage of the MEM has docked with its mother ship in orbit, the astronauts will transfer their surface samples, then leave the MEM themselves. During this procedure a continuous flow of air will move from the airlock of the mission module into the MEM. This will keep any Martian dust from getting into the interplanetary spacecraft.

AT THE SPEED OF SOUND: This little metal cone is traveling at just about the speed of sound, 740 mph, in simulated Martian atmosphere during tests at NASA's Ames Research Center. (NASA Photo)

After the astronauts and all the surface samples are aboard the mission module, any trash that has accumulated during the flight will be dumped into the MEM. Even with a completely closed ecology there are bound to be some wastes—such as used note paper and empty food bags. The abandoned MEM will now be cut loose from the interplanetary spacecraft and either be left in orbit around Mars or sent crashing down to the Martian surface. The latter would provide shock waves so that the seismograph can reveal the inner structure of Mars.

6 Down to Venus

Their investigation of Mars completed, the interplanetary expedition will head homeward. On this return trip a slower flight would have one advantage. It would allow the astronauts to spend their quarantine time aboard the spacecraft. This is the period needed to see if the astronauts have contracted any harmful diseases on Mars.

A synodic or Venus flyby mission would provide more than ample time for quarantine. Even the fast thirty-day trip possible with a gaseous-core reactor would be enough for the minimum quarantine time. However, with a photon rocket the astronauts would be back to Earth as quickly as astronauts returning from the moon now. Thus, they would have to spend the remaining weeks of their quarantine in isolation on Earth.

If the first flights to Mars are made by solid-core or gaseous core reactors, the quarantine problem will have been eliminated by the time the photon rockets are flying. It may be found that the Martian bacteria are of no danger to humans, or if they are, it will be a relatively simple matter to develop a vaccine. The first step in this process, the isolation of the germs, will be automatic.

Of course, steps will be taken to eliminate any Martian bacteria that get loose in the mission module. Bacteria filters will strain them out as the air and water are passed through the recycling system. If any astronauts do come down with Martian germs—or any Earthly ailments—the expedition's physician will have a full supply of antibiotics and other drugs to treat them.

Solar flares may give the astronauts some help in cleaning off the hitchhiking germs. These powerful bursts of solar radiation will kill any organisms riding in unprotected parts of the spacecraft. However, protection will be needed and will be provided for the astronauts and for other living things that must survive the flight.

Since weight is always at a premium on a spacecraft, it would be better if the manned interplanetary spaceflights were launched when the solar flares were at a minimum. The turbulence in the sun's atmosphere, including solar flares, will reach a peak twice in the remainder of the twentieth century—in 1980 and 1991. If an interplanetary spacecraft were launched halfway between these eleven-year peaks, it would encounter few, if any, solar flares.

This works out nicely for the expedition scheduled to visit Mars during the close opposition on July 10, 1986. There would not be much more danger of solar flares on a flight to Venus during its September, 1983, inferior conjunction. However, the next inferior conjunction comes in 1991—right at the peak of solar activity.

During the trip to Mars and Venus observatories on Earth will keep a watch for solar flares. Whenever one of these flares is sighted, a warning will be sent to the interplanetary expedition. Solar flares travel slower than light, so astronomers can see them coming. When an astronomer sees the bright spot of a solar flare appear on the sun's surface, he knows that an explosion has just sent a cloud of ions streaming out from the sun.

The leading edge of this ion cloud will reach Mercury in 3.9 to 23.4 minutes, pass Venus in 7.2 to 43.2 minutes, Earth in 10 to 60 minutes, and Mars in 15.2 to 91.2 minutes. This means that the astronauts aboard the interplanetary spacecraft will have between 3.9 and 87.04 minutes to prepare for the ion cloud, depending on where they are at the time and how fast the cloud is traveling.

Warnings from Earth will come in plenty of time—until a manned expedition nears Mercury. It will then take at least 4.88 minutes for a message to reach the spacecraft. So the astronauts will then have to stand their own solar watch.

Obviously this will be done with special solar telescopes since the sun is too bright to be viewed directly even at Earth's distance from the sun. Actually, the expedition's astronomer will be using these telescopes throughout the mission to study the sun from angles and distances that cannot be obtained by observatories on Earth or in Earth orbit.

When a solar flare is due, the astronauts will don polyethylene coveralls with water-filled linings and plastic helmets to protect them from radiation. Water-filled blankets will also be thrown over the greenhouse and cultures of Martian organisms. The fish are already well protected in their watery environment.

The ion cloud will pass over the spacecraft in a few hours. Only rarely does a solar flare last more than a day or two at the most. When the danger is past, the astronauts can remove their protective clothing, fold away the water-filled blankets, and return to more routine life.

Solar flares will only be part of the radiation that will bombard the spacecraft. There will also be a continuous stream of particles from the sun and cosmic rays from space. The hull of the mission module must shield the astronauts from these rays. A layer of polyethylene in the spacecraft's inner hull would serve this purpose. For fire protection this would be lined by incombustible materials, probably fluorocarbon plastics and fiberglass. These will be better than aluminum because when cosmic rays hit metal, they knock loose new particles called secondary cosmic rays.

The closer the spacecraft approaches to the sun, the more radiation shielding it will need. Twice as much will be needed near Venus as in Earth orbit. By the time a manned spacecraft reaches Mercury it will need five to ten times the radiation shielding it did in Earth orbit. It all depends on whether Mercury is at the aphelion (closest to the sun) or perihelion (farthest from the sun) of its unusually elliptical orbit.

Not all the solar radiation will be a hazard to the expedi-

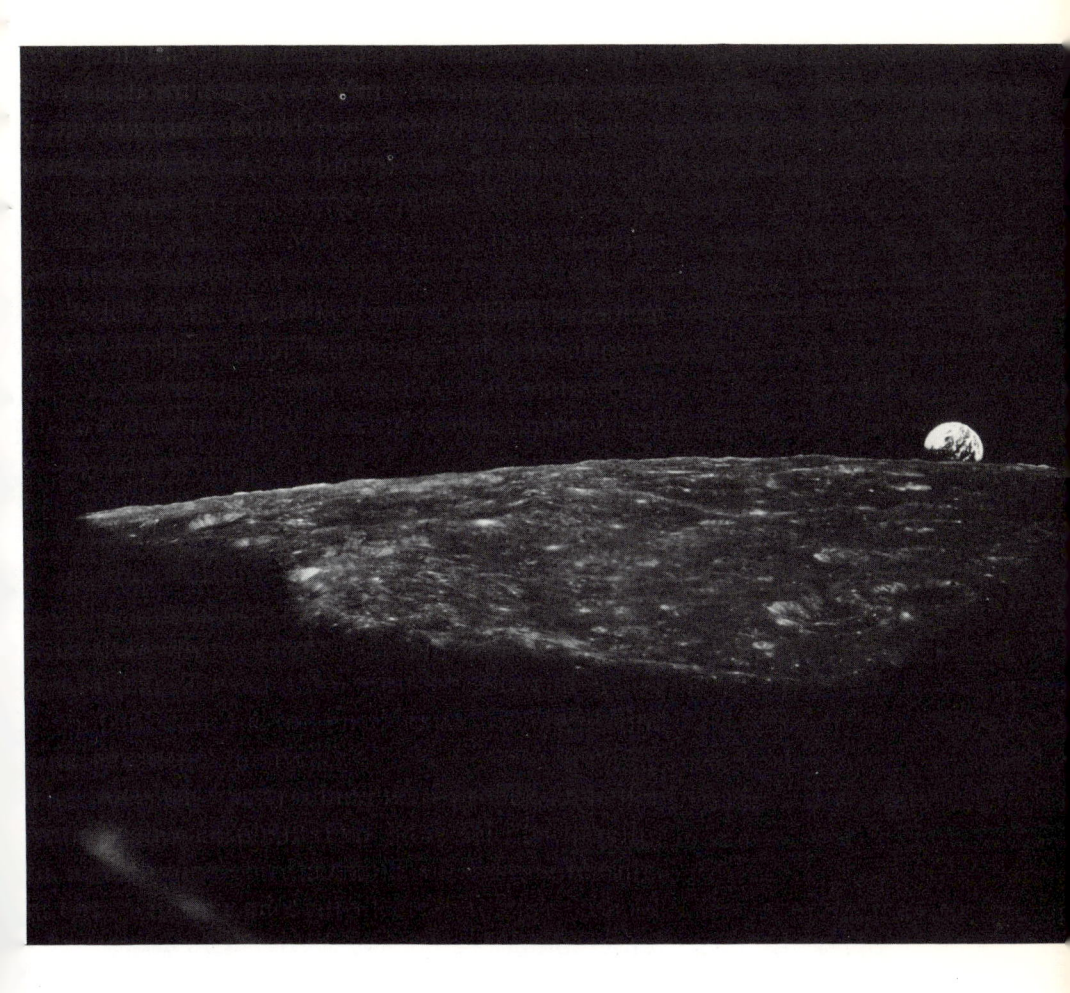

APOLLO 8 EARTH VIEW: The sun as seen from Mercury would be much the size the Earth appears in this photograph taken by the Apollo 8 astronauts. Of course, the sun would be so bright it could not in fact be viewed or photographed directly. (NASA Photo by Apollo 8 astronauts distributed by Movie Newsreels)

tion. Some of it will be a help. If the interplanetary spacecraft receives its electrical power from solar batteries, increasing sunlight would cause these batteries to generate more and more power as the spacecraft neared the sun.

This makes possible another method of shielding the spacecraft from radiation. It could use powerful electric magnets to generate a magnetic field which would protect the spacecraft from radiation just as Earth's magnetic field protects us.

There will, however, be no magnetic field to protect the astronauts when they visit Mars or Venus.

The first manned visit to Venus will probably be a fly-by on the return from Mars. This first quick glance will provide only a tantalizing look at the mysteries of Venus—like seeing the previews of a movie. To uncover more of Venus' secrets, a later manned expedition will have to go into orbit about Venus.

From a few thousand miles' altitude Venus will be a truly dazzling sight for the astronauts. Almost as large as Earth, Venus reflects nearly three times as much light as their home planet. No alien surface features will be seen by the astronauts, however, for it is a great mass of slightly yellowish clouds that gives Venus its brilliance.

In spite of this, there is quite a bit that can be gained by observing and photographing Venus. As Merton E. Davies and Bruce C. Murray explain in *The View from Space:* "... useful information concerning cloud heights and shapes, perhaps bearing on atmospheric structure and dynamics, may be available from close-up visible photography along the terminator [line between night and day] and the limb [horizon]."

NEW CONCEPT: Preliminary design for a Mars mission Earth re-entry vehicle conceived by the Lockheed Missiles & Space Company. (Lockheed Aircraft Corp.)

Besides photographing Venus in visible light the astronauts will study the planet in infrared (heat) and ultraviolet radiation. In the infrared the astronauts will record the temperatures and gases above the 35-mile-high clouds. With ultraviolet photography they will seek an answer to why the ultraviolet markings on Venus appear to rotate every four to five days—more than fifty times as fast as the surface.

To find out what lies beneath the clouds, the astronauts will probe the Venutian atmosphere with microwave and radar beams. The microwave beams will show the temperatures beneath the clouds and the composition of Venus' lower atmosphere. The radar will map the surface features of Venus more accurately than radar beams from Earth.

Unmanned spacecraft will also be sent down to Venus from the interplanetary expedition. These probes could either parachute to the surface or release balloons and float in the clouds. Perhaps one will be sent to the surface and the other to float in the clouds.

The probe that goes to the Venutian surface will be descending into a world unlike any ever imagined by anyone on Earth. The thick atmosphere of Venus presses down with 100 times the pressure of Earth's atmosphere or about what it is half a mile beneath the sea. It is made up of 95 percent carbon dioxide and traps the heat of the sun, so temperatures at the surface of Venus climb as high as 1,000° F.

Even at night there is no relief from the heat. The United States' Mariner probes have reported the same temperatures all over Venus. This leads many astronomers to speculate that there may be winds of hurricane force blowing about Venus, distributing the heat all over that planet. These winds would whip up dust storms, adding to the turbidity of the atmosphere and increasing its greenhouse effect. There may also be volcanoes belching out more heat and smoke into the air, making the climate still more unbearable.

If the probe's television cameras could penetrate Venus' clouds, they would show a very strange world indeed. The landscape would appear to be shaped like a bowl rather than flat as it appears on Earth. There would be only a few mountains to be seen through the fog. Strange lakes of molten aluminum, bismuth, lead, tin, and magnesium, as well as liquid acetic acid and benzene, might dot the land.

A strange sunset would end the long Venutian day. The sun would appear to dissolve as it dropped low in the eastern horizon. A glow would then spread around the horizon and linger until the sun appeared to recondense on the western horizon at the start of a new day.

The probe that floats in the atmosphere of Venus will find a much more hospitable climate. NASA's Mariner probes have reported that the temperatures at the tops of Venus' clouds is $-35°$ F. Somewhere between this freezing upper air and the scorching surface of Venus there must be a level which life could stand.

One thing the floating probe will be looking for is water vapor. Some probes of Venus have reported abundant water in that planet's clouds, while others have found little, if any.

It is also possible that the probe could find living

organisms floating in the Venutian atmosphere, like plankton in Earthly seas. Balloons have found microorganisms floating in the upper air of Earth where they are buffeted by 100-mile-per-hour winds like those on Venus. Some Earth organisms are also living without water or oxygen so similar ones might exist in the clouds of Venus.

While it might be possible to devise a manned spacecraft that could safely land and take off from Venus, no astronaut could step out on the surface even wearing a space suit. If an astronaut ventured outside the haven of his spacecraft at all, it would have to be in a thick-walled capsule much like those used for exploring the ocean depths. To pick up surface samples, he would have to use mechanical arms like those used in atomic plants.

It would be much simpler to send these manipulators to the surface of Venus aboard an unmanned spacecraft and operate them by radio control from the interplanetary spacecraft. Television pictures would show the astronauts what they were doing. By using image enhancers like those used on television pictures sent back by Apollo astronauts on the moon, the astronauts could probably see more clearly with these electronic "eyes" than they could with their own.

For mobility the cameras and manipulators would be mounted on a small rover resembling the Russians' Lunakhod moon explorer. Under the direction of the orbiting astronauts this remote-controlled robot would collect rock and air samples.

Meanwhile, floating probes high in Venus' atmosphere would also be collecting air samples. Both probes would seal the samples in airtight containers and place them aboard rockets to be launched into orbit.

It will take almost as much fuel to lift off into orbit around Venus as it does to go into Earth orbit because Venus' gravity is .91 of Earth's gravity. Obviously the fuel chosen for the rocket that carries samples from the surface will have to not vaporize or ignite under the heat and pressure on Venus until time for launch.

UNLOADING THE LANDER: If there is no atmosphere on Mercury, the scene of the landing party unloading their equipment by the light of Venus would look much like this artist's concept of a space tug being unloaded on the moon. (Grumman Aerospace Corp.)

7 Stopover at Mercury

Just as the manned expedition to Mars flew by Venus on the return to Earth, the flight to Venus could stop over at Mercury on the way back to Earth.

As the manned spacecraft approach Mercury, their defenses against the increasing heat and radiation will be put to the test. The panels of solar batteries will be tilted so that the sunlight no longer falls directly on them. They will still provide plenty of power, but they will not be damaged by the sun. Mirrors could also be interspersed with the solar batteries to radiate some of the heat back into space. The spacecraft's Inconel X hull will also be mirror-surfaced for the same purpose. Any heat that soaks through this barrier will be absorbed by liquid nitrogen or some similar cold fluid, carried off to the dark side of the spacecraft and radiated back into space.

Astronomers on Earth have been able to discover little about the surface of Mercury because that planet orbits so close to the sun that it is usually lost in that star's glare. In 1965 radar studies of Mercury by Dr. Gordon H. Pettengill showed another handicap to observations of that planet. Dr. Pettengill found that Mercury's rotation is 58.65 days long. This works out to two-thirds of the planet's 88-day-long year. Thus Mercury nearly always turns the same face toward Earth.

To the astronauts who visit Mercury it will be a much more familiar place than it is to us today. They will have studied photographs and other information sent back by unmanned probes of that planet. As with Mars, flyby probes are the first step; then come orbiting probes and finally unmanned landings.

Besides photographing the mysterious surface of Mercury, the unmanned probes must answer several other riddles before a manned expedition can even be planned. One of these was answered by Mariner 10. This was: does Mercury have an atmosphere? Because of its small size, Mercury should never have had anything but a thin atmosphere and this should have been boiled away long ago by the fierce rays of the sun.

However, Mercury's indistinct markings are sometimes obscured for viewers on Earth as if by a dust storm like those on Mars. Still these could have been caused by escaping gas clouds like those that sometimes appear on the moon or even by shimmering in the Earth's atmosphere. Thus astronomer Edward Reeves of Harvard didn't quite believe it when he found that some of the data recorded by Skylab as Mercury passed in front of the sun, called a transit, showed that this planet had an atmosphere.

When it flew past Mercury on March 25, 1974, Mariner 10 confirmed Skylab's finding of an atmosphere on that planet. The probe found that Mercury's atmosphere is made up mostly of helium. This may either have been captured from the solar wind, a constant stream of radiation from the sun, or by radioactive elements in Mercury. There is also some neon and possibly also a little xenon trapped from the solar wind in Mercury's atmosphere. Another gas, argon, appears to have come from radioactive elements on Mercury.

This atmosphere is not an even layer over the planet's surface as are most atmospheres. It streams out behind Mercury like the tail of a comet. Mercury's atmosphere is only about one hundred-billionth as dense as Earth's air and only extends out to 300 miles above the planet. This is much too thin to be used to slow the Mercury lander as it nears the planet. This means that the landing craft will have to use rocket power for the entire descent, as did the Apollo Lunar Modules.

The Mercury lander will probably resemble an enlarged version of the space tug equipped with Apollo Lunar Module-like landing gear. NASA has proposed a moon landing model of the space tug to put three astronauts on the moon for up to twenty-eight days of exploring. The Mercury lander, however, would carry six men and be prepared for a forty-day stay on that planet. This spacecraft would have to carry four times as much fuel as a space tug because of the higher gravity on Mercury. Of course, it would also need an Inconel X outer hull and cooling system like the interplanetary spacecraft.

Whichever way must be used for the landing on Mercury, the astronauts will set down in surroundings that bear a striking similarity to the medieval ideas of hell. For instance, in *Voices from the Sky* Arthur C. Clarke says, "Above any valleys on the day side of Mercury, the Sun could hang almost vertically overhead forever, while its rays—ten times as powerful as on Earth—reverberated from the surrounding walls. From such valleys might flow rivers of molten metal, seeking, as do rivers on Earth, their own infernal seas."

Clarke wrote this before 1965, when astronomers were certain that Mercury always kept one face toward the sun, just as the moon turns one face toward Earth. Nevertheless, there is still enough heat on Mercury's sunlight side to create the molten metal rivers and seas Clarke envisioned.

Aside from these un-Earthly seas and rivers, the astronauts will find the Mercurian landscape much like that of the moon and probably just as lifeless. No known form of living organism could survive the heat and radiation of a day on Mercury.

The manned landing will be made on the western edge of the day side of Mercury. Before setting foot on the surface, the astronauts must wait until the temperatures moderate after sundown. However, if the landing is made when Mercury is at perihelion, the sun will seem unable to make up its mind.

The brilliant orb, appearing three times as large as it does from Earth, would first set, then rise briefly, and

BIG DISH: This huge antenna at Goldstone, California, and others like it around the world will track manned interplanetary flights as they now follow unmanned probes. (NASA Photo)

finally sink below the horizon for the night. This night will last for 88 days, for Mercury's rotation and its revolution combine to give it a solar day (from noon to noon) of 176 Earth days—exactly twice the length of its year.

Once the sun has set, its heat escapes rapidly from the thin atmosphere of Mercury. The shimmering metal rivers gradually become sluggish and then frozen. Within a few Earth days the temperature has plummeted to 200 degrees below zero. By morning it is down to nearly $-280°$ F—a drop of over $1,000°$ F, the greatest on any planet in the solar system.

Actually this cold is only thirty degrees lower than the $-250°$ temperatures the space suits worn by the Apollo astronauts were equipped to handle, and these will probably be considered old-fashioned by the astronauts who visit Mercury. Thus, for the first few Earth days after nightfall the Mercury explorers will be comfortable outside in just their normal spacesuits. Later in the night, however, they might want to put on a sweater and heavier trousers under their space suits.

Keeping warm inside a spacesuit isn't really too much of a problem even during the Mercurian night. This is because the spacesuit contains its own ever-efficient heater—the human body which, of course, operates at around $98.6°$. However, body heat is not enough to keep the Mercury lander warm. It will obviously need a heater. The same steam heating system that would work for the Mars excursion module would also serve the Mercury lander. It would only have to run more steadily, which it is perfectly capable of doing.

Mercury's atmosphere will be no problem for the astronauts, especially if the lander has an oxygen-helium atmosphere. Any helium that might get into the cabin of the lander through the airlock will simply mix with the rest of the craft's atmosphere. Of course, the Mercury explorers will take precautions against tracking dust into the cabin, just as their predecessors on the moon and Mars did. Besides preventing any germs that might somehow have survived on Mercury from getting into the cabin, this will also help to keep things neat.

In spite of its thinness, Mercury's atmosphere may have one advantage for the astronauts. Its upper limits may contain a layer of electrically charged particles, called ions. Although this ionosphere would be very weak, the astronauts might be able to use it to reflect radio messages over the horizon just as we use Earth's much stronger ionosphere.

The astronauts will carry out research on Mercury similar to that done by their predecessors on Mars. This time, however, the exo-biologist's main task will be to see if any organic compounds have developed in spite of the harsh conditions on Mercury.

The geologist meanwhile will be examining the rocks on Mercury for uranium and thorium. Meanwhile, too, the meteorologist will measure the density, air currents and composition of Mercury's thin atmosphere. These studies will help to determine whether Mercury's atmosphere comes from the sun or from radioactive elements within the planet.

If Mercury's atmosphere comes from radioactive elements, the geologist should have an easy time locating uranium and thorium. Astronomer Michael B. McElroy of Harvard thinks there may be as much uranium and thorium on Mercury as there is on Earth.

During their forty-day stay on the night side of Mercury the astronauts will need substitutes for the vitamin D which they would normally receive through sunlight. This can be obtained either through fish-liver oil, egg yolk, butter, or ultra violet lights or through some combination of these.

The night on Mercury will hardly be dark, for the Earth will be shining down with the brilliance of a full moon. If Venus is in the sky, it will add a light of four times that of the full moon. Earth and Venus combined will still not give nearly as much light as the sun does on Earth, or even on Mars. Still, they are bright enough that the astronauts will not need lights except to look into the shadows.

Special fast films are also available for photography in light levels such as would be found on Mercury. Also, by the time of the manned flight to Mercury television cameras that can "see" as well as the human eye will probably have been developed.

As the end of their stay on Mercury approaches, the astronauts will stow away their sealed boxes of Mercury rocks and throw out the overshoes and other equipment used in exploring the planet. They will then lift off in the ascent stage of the Mercury lander and rejoin their companions in orbit.

If the landing had been made when Mercury was at perihelion, that planet will have moved to aphelion by the time the landing party rejoins the interplanetary spacecraft. Thus, when the astronauts see the sun again, its apparent size will have shrunk to only twice as large as it appears from Earth.

When the astronauts and their Mercury samples are aboard the interplanetary spacecraft, they will use the Mercury lander as a trash can and then abandon it as they head back to Earth. Later, if bases are established on Mars or Mercury, reusable landing rockets will be needed.

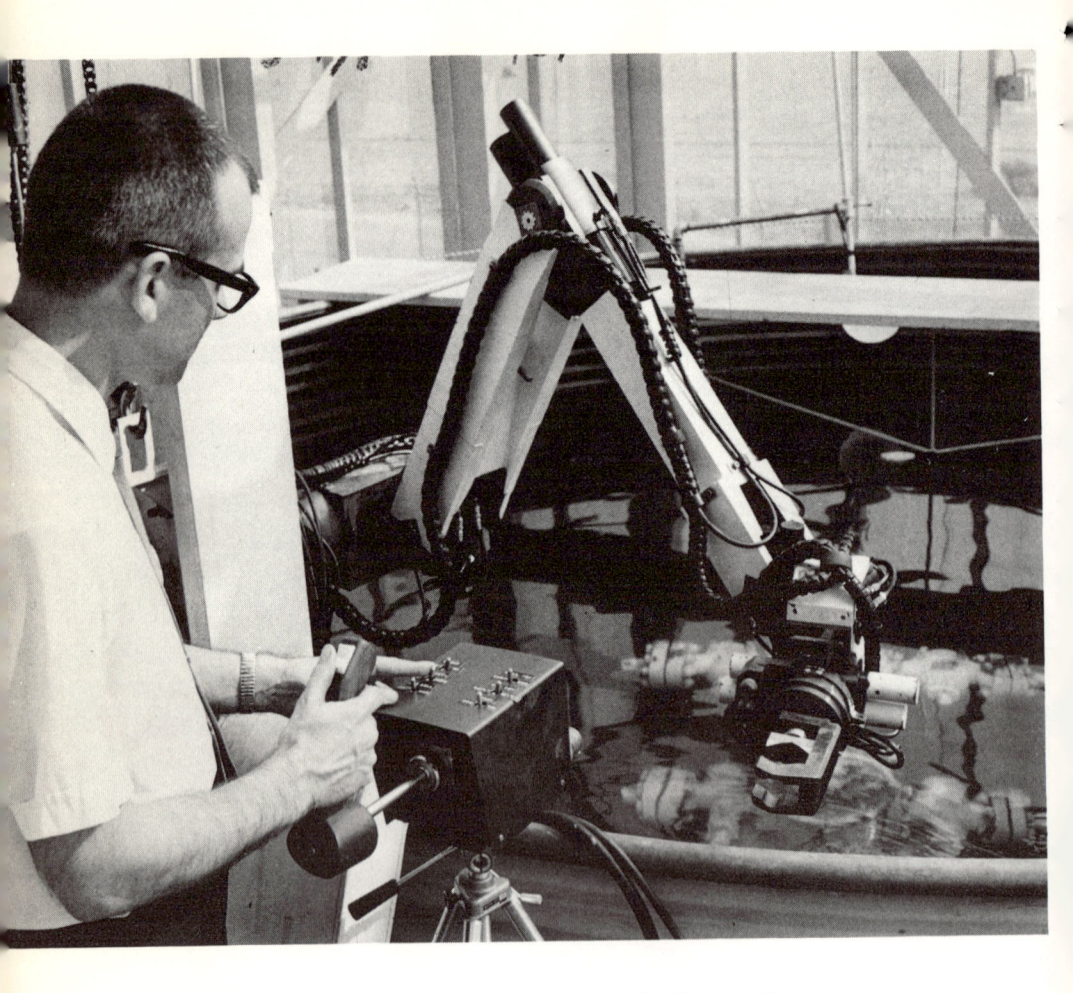

REMOTE MANIPULATOR: Manipulators similar to this one developed for deep sea use could be adapted for working on Venus. On that planet they would need heat protection and would have to be operated by radio control rather than cables. (North American Rockwell, Ocean Systems Operation)

8 Return to Earth

During the return trip to Earth the astronauts will begin the preliminary studies of the data they have collected on Mars and Venus or on Venus and Mercury, depending on the mission. If there is a darkroom aboard the spacecraft, the astronauts might even develop some of the films they have taken. They will also continue their studies of space between the planets.

One experiment which could be performed on the interplanetary flights will not be finished until the astronauts have returned to Earth orbit. This would be a check of Einstein's special theory of relativity which indicates that time will move more slowly the faster an object travels. Even at the fastest practical interplanetary speeds this would amount to only a few fractions of a second. For example, a photon rocket making a three-day flight to Mars would lose less than .0005 of a second. On slower flights it would be much less than this.

Nevertheless, this small change could be detected by using extremely accurate atomic clocks. One of these would be carried by the spacecraft and compared with an identical clock left on Earth. A similar experiment was carried out by astronomer Richard Keating and physicist Joseph C. Hafele in October, 1971, using jet planes.

If the interplanetary spacecraft has artificial gravity, the atomic clock will probably be placed in the axle so that the mission module's rotation will not confuse the calculations. There will be enough other motions to take into account. The interplanetary spacecraft will not be traveling at a constant rate of speed. All the changes in speed will have to be taken into account, whether they come from firing the rocket engines or from the gravities of the sun and planets. Data on all these things will be fed into a computer to aid in determining the time change during the interplanetary flight.

This information may prove to be of more than purely scientific importance. If colonies are ever established on the planets, the colonists will want atomic clocks to check the accuracy of more conventional clocks, just as is done on Earth. In order to do this, they will need to know what effect the trip has had on the atomic clock. Knowing the precise time is also important in navigating the spacecraft.

The interplanetary spacecraft will carry an inertial guidance system. This is an instrument which contains three spinning gyroscopes, each of which continually points toward the same point in space. By measuring the changing angles of these gyros, the astronauts and the spacecraft's computer can tell their position.

Meanwhile, back on Earth huge, dish-shaped antennas will be tracking the interplanetary spacecraft by means of the radio messages it sends back. Flight controllers can report this information to the astronauts to back up the inertial-guidance system. However, as the spacecraft travels farther and farther from Earth, it will take longer and longer for these messages to reach it.

Thus the astronauts will have to determine their own position by the stars as a check on the inertial-guidance system. The navigator will take sightings on the target planet and three bright stars. He will then note the exact time of the sighting and the angle between the planet and stars.

From this he will be able to project three imaginary cones in space. The point at which the cones intercept will be the exact location of the spacecraft. This position will then be compared with the place the spacecraft should be at this moment in the flight. If there is any difference in the two, the spacecraft's rockets will be fired for a short time to correct it.

As the spacecraft nears its target, the planet's appearance will change from a point of light to a disk. The navigator will then have to make his sightings on a landmark on the planet's surface. In the case of Venus, where there are no landmarks visible, he will use the point at which the terminator (line between the day and night sides) and the limb (edge of the disk) intersect. This might also be helpful on the approach to Earth, where clouds obscure most of the landmarks.

During its mission a NERVA-powered interplanetary spacecraft will have used up about 1,410,000 pounds of weight. This includes the two boosters which sent it off on its journey, the landing craft, and about 640,000 pounds of fuel and other consumables. Of the remaining 190,000 pounds about 30,000 will be fuel needed to return to Earth orbit.

If this fuel were replaced by a heat shield, the spacecraft could make a reentry and landing like an Apollo command module. Still more fuel could be saved by using the upper fringes of other planets' atmospheres to go into orbit. Instead of being basically a long cylinder, such a spacecraft would be a cone, like the Apollo command module, only about eight times its size.

The only drawback to such a design is that after reentry the interplanetary spacecraft would have to be refurbished and then returned to orbit by Saturn V for another mission. Obviously it would be much more convenient to put a returning interplanetary spacecraft into a parking orbit and leave it there until it is needed again.

The faster a spacecraft returns to Earth, the more heat shielding it will need for reentry. For example, a spacecraft returning at 47,000 miles per hour would need to be 50 percent heat shield in order to survive reentry. However, the amount of fuel needed to go into parking orbit would not increase because more efficient rockets would be used for these faster trips.

Even though an interplanetary spacecraft would ordinarily return to Earth orbit, it could carry a small Earth

TAKING STAR SIGHTINGS: Standing in a mock-up of an Apollo spacecraft, a technician shows how an astronaut uses a sextant to take sightings on stars. The sextant has been used by navigators for centuries. (Martin Company)

entry module (EEM) which would serve as a lifeboat if the main rocket engine failed at the last moment.

The Lockheed Missiles and Space Company has designed an EEM which could be used for reentries at speeds up to 44,317 miles per hour. This craft is made of two broad double cones base to base and resembles a flying saucer. It is designed solely to bring back four to six astronauts, plus 800 pounds of equipment and samples from the planets. If one of the two interplanetary spacecraft were to be abandoned earlier in the flight, its crew would have to bring their EEM along when they transferred to the other ship.

Of course, the astronauts would not give up on starting the main engine of their interplanetary spacecraft on the first try, but if all attempts failed, they would be forced to abandon ship. They would strap themselves into their couches in the EEM, run quickly through a checklist of the equipment, and then separate from the disabled interplanetary spacecraft.

Even though this would be an emergency landing, it will have been carefully prepared for, like everything else in any spaceflight. The astronauts will have practiced this abort maneuver many times in simulators, and during the flight they will hold lifeboat drills to make sure that the equipment in the EEM is working properly and to keep themselves familiar with the procedures needed for the abort.

As soon as the interplanetary spacecraft has made its final mid-course correction, the site of a possible emergency landing will be selected and a recovery force sent there just in case it is needed. If it does have to be used, its role will be the same as that of the recovery forces in the Apollo program.

The EEM will hit the atmosphere at an altitude of 400,000 feet, and air friction will quickly create a heat of 45,000° F. The 3½-inch-thick layer of ablative material will boil away, carrying with it all but 300° F of the heat. This remaining heat will be walled out by the main hull of the spacecraft—a stainless-steel sandwich.

At about 200,000 feet the EEM will have slowed enough for the astronauts to level off and head for their landing site. For this maneuver the astronauts will fire steering rockets, rolling the EEM to control the lift given by its shape.

The possible landing sites for the EEM would stretch out before it in an area shaped like a giant footprint 1,150 miles wide and 18,400 miles long. Within this landing footprint the astronauts can choose any landing site from California's Mojave Desert to Woomera, Australia.

After making its reentry, the EEM will release parachutes to cushion its landing or splashdown. The recovery forces will be watching this, and helicopters will be waiting when the EEM finally comes to rest.

Even if it is never needed for an emergency landing, the EEM will not just go along for the ride. The EEM's broad heat shield will serve as part of the interplanetary spacecraft's antiradiation armor. If the EEM's were equipped with small propulsion rockets, as well as steering jets, they could be used to go between the interplanetary spacecraft during the flight, just as boats are used on the sea.

If no emergency reentry is needed, the interplanetary spacecraft will enter parking orbit. Here it will probably rendezvous and dock at the space station where the crew members received their training for the flight. According to NASA's latest studies, this will be a huge space base staffed by 100 scientists from all over the world. The Russians have shown sketches of a similar space station.

Both the Soviet and American space station would have to be launched in sections and docked together in orbit, just as the interplanetary spacecraft would be. However, in this case the construction would probably be much slower, lasting over several years. NASA's space base would begin as a six-man space station. Over a period of ten years or more additional modules would be added until it grew into a huge space base.

At the U.S. space base or the Soviet space station, the returning interplanetary astronauts will receive more complete medical examinations than could be given by the expedition's physician. They will also receive their first debriefing and possibly even be interviewed by the press. If any quarantine time is needed, the interplanetary astronauts will spend it in an isolation chamber at one end of the space base.

When they are ready to return to Earth, the astronauts will board one of the space base's regular supply rockets. This will either be two of NASA's space shuttles or some similar reusable spacecraft. In 1964 NASA began a study of the possibility of a four- to six-man space station. Originally this station was to be supplied by Gemini or Apollo spacecraft. However, it was soon found that these nonreusable spacecraft were far too expensive, so the concept of the reusable space shuttle was born. If the Russians begin designing a permanent space station, they will find that they also need a reusable supply rocket.

Thus, for the interplanetary astronauts the end of their mission will come when the space shuttle carrying them reenters the atmosphere and glides in for a landing on a jet runway. On this last leg of their trip the interplanetary astronauts will just be passengers. The shuttles' regular crews will handle the flying of those craft.

No doubt when the space shuttles carrying the interplanetary astronauts touch down, either the President of the United States or the Premier of the Soviet Union—or both—will be on hand to greet the returning astronauts. Since manned interplanetary missions require two spacecraft, they are naturals for cooperation between the United States and the Soviet Union. Other nations might also join in the mission. However, in the past international competition rather than cooperation has been the biggest spur to space exploration.

The samples brought back by the interplanetary spacecraft will probably remain at the space station some time after the interplanetary astronauts have returned to Earth. Aboard the space station there will be less chance of the precious samples, being contaminated by earthly substances. Also, the scientists at the station will be able to perform more extensive tests than the astronauts were able to during their return flight.

Only when these tests are completed will a shuttle rocket

deliver the planetary samples to Earth. More tests will then follow, and finally, some of the samples will be placed on public display.

The interplanetary spacecraft will remain docked at the space station or floating nearby. Their equipment would be shut down until time to prepare for another mission. Since the first few interplanetary flights will be timed to arrive at their target planet when it is closest to Earth, the waiting time between missions will depend on how fast the interplanetary spacecraft can travel. For a NERVA-powered spacecraft there would be practically no waiting time at all, while there would be a wait of nearly two years for a gaseous-core reactor or photon-rocket-powered spacecraft.

This means that a NERVA-powered interplanetary spacecraft will need a completely new crew for its second mission since the first team of astronauts will have earned a vacation on Earth. If there is no artificial gravity aboard the interplanetary spacecraft, the astronauts will probably also need some time to recover from the effects of weightlessness.

A new crew would also be needed if the second mission were to visit a different planet from the one visited on the first flight. It would be too much to expect the astronauts to become experts on three planets, as well as to fly between them. Instead, one crew would be trained to fly to Mars and Venus and investigate them, while the other crew would be trained to fly to Venus and Mercury and investigate those planets.

Although separate crews would be needed for the Mars landing-Venus flyby and the Bikini mission the same spacecraft could serve on both. Of course, the Inconel X hull and heavy radiation shielding required near Mercury would not be needed on the flight to Mars and Venus. However, carrying it along would cost less than assembling two new spacecraft for the Bikini mission.

The liquid nitrogen coolant to be used in the vicinity of Mercury would not have to be carried along on the Mars trip. It could be added before the Bikini mission, just as antifreeze is added to a car's radiator before winter. Also, before a new mission any equipment that had failed during the previous flight would be replaced. Some obsolete equipment would also be replaced by improved systems.

To make this replacement simpler, the equipment aboard the interplanetary spacecraft could be designed to plug in, like appliances on Earth. A similar system was used in the Gemini and Apollo spacecraft, as well as the orbiting observatory satellites. With the greater space aboard the interplanetary spacecraft the process of changing systems can be made even simpler.

Among the new equipment added to the interplanetary spacecraft will be a new landing craft and unmanned planetary probes. These, too, will probably include a number of changes found necessary after the first flight. The changes will be both in improved systems and in equipment added to investigate puzzles raised by the previous mission.

When the refurbishment of the interplanetary spacecraft is completed, they will be refueled and taken on shakedown cruises around the moon. As before, these test flights will be made first with the interplanetary spacecraft themselves. Finally, the fuel and other consumables will be loaded aboard the interplanetary spacecraft, and when the proper time arrives, another flight to the planets will begin.

Just as Apollo 11 was not the only moon landing but the first of many, so there will be repeated visits to Mars, Venus, and Mercury. With replacement of the worn-out and obsolete parts the interplanetary spacecraft that made the first flight can make many of the subsequent ones.

In fact, since the interplanetary spacecraft is made up of modules, the entire mission module or propulsion module could be replaced. For example, to add a more efficient rocket engine, the old propulsion module would be undocked from the mission module and a new one docked in its place.

Of course, space explorers will probably not be content with visiting just the inner planets. Beyond Mars is a belt of countless tiny planets called asteroids, and beyond this are four giant planets with twenty-seven satellites. Four of these satellites are larger than our own moon, and one is as large as Mercury. Orbiting on the very edge of the solar system is a small cold planet, Pluto. Then, beyond a void which even light takes years to cross, there are the stars, which may have still other planets circling them.

Exploring all these worlds beyond Mars will present a host of new problems. However, these puzzles are even now being solved. An unmanned probe, Pioneer 10, has already been launched to Jupiter, the first and largest of the giant planets. Manned spaceflight to Mars, Venus, and Mercury will provide another long step in the exploration of space.

Index

Air: in space, 9–10; in spacecraft, 61, 62, 64, 65–66, 68
Aldrin, Edwin E. "Buz," 37, 40
Aphelion, 92, 108
Apollo program, 10, 46, 80; flashfire, 68; spacecraft, 16, 25–26, 64, 114
Aristarchus (moon crater), 50
Astronautics and Aeronautics, 33–34
Astronauts: decompression problem, 62, 64-65, 66, 68; duties, 72; Earth emergency entry, 116; exercise, 58; and g's, 35; and germs, 84, 90; Mars exploration, 73-88; Mercury exploration, 102–9; pilot, 46, 72, 82; recovery time between missions, 120; scientist, 46, 72, 84-85; space hazards, 20, 30–32; space suits, 106; weightlessness, 53–54, 56, 58, Venus exploration, 94–99. *See also* Crew of spacecraft
Astronomer, 72, 91, 107–08
Atomic clocks, 112
Atomic Energy Commission (AEC), 30

Bacteria, problem of, 84-85, 90, 107

Bikini mission, 22-23, 43, 120-21
Biological clocks. *See* Circadian rhythm
Boredom, problem of, 72

Carbon suboxide, on Mars, 85
Carson, Robert K., 85
Circadian rhythm, 62
Clarke, Arthur C., 66–68, 104
Closed ecology. *See* Ecology, closed
Cobra Head (moon plain), 50
Crew of spacecraft, 23, 25, 119, 120; experience and training, 43, 46, 72, 111. *See also* Astronauts
Cycle of oppositions. *See* Oppositions, cycle of

Davies, Merton E., 94
Decompression problem, 65–68

Earth: atmosphere, 10, 64; and gravity, 17–18; Mercury inferior conjunction, 23; microorganisms, 98; and navigation, to, 113; oppositions, 14; orbit, 18, 19, 37; Venus inferior conjunctions, 16. *See also* Emergency entry module.

125

Ecology, closed, 58, 60, 61
Ehricke, Dr. Krafft A., 17
Einstein, Albert. *See* Relativity, theory of
Emergency entry module (EEM), 116–17
Exobiologist, 84–85, 107
Exploration of Space (Clarke), 66–68

Fertilizer, use of, 70
Fire problem, 68–69
Flyby flight, 16–17. *See also* Venus, flyby
Food, 58, 70
Fuel. *See* Propellant
Fusion reactor power rocket, 32–34

Gaseous-core nuclear rocket, 32–33, 36, 89, 120
Gemini program, 37, 40, 118, 121
Geologist, 85, 107
Glenn, John, 60
Gravity, 17, 18, 19, 35; artificial, 53–56, 58, 69, 73, 112, 120; gravity assist, 21; and Mars and Mercury, 48

Hafele, Joseph C., 112
Heat shielding, 114, 117
Helium, 64–65, 103
Hibernation, 70, 72, 103

Inconel X, 22, 101, 104, 121
Inertial guidance system. *See* Navigation
Inferior conjunction, 16, 23

Keating, Richard, 112

Launch window, 17, 22

Manned orbital laboratories, (MOL), 64
Mariner program, 76, 96–97, 102–03
Mars, 10, 13, 65, 111–12; characteristics, 48, 74, 78, 80, 82, 85, 86; crew and craft, 23, 120–22; exploration of, 73–88; moons of, 82; oppositions cycle, 14, 90; and solar flares, 91–92; travel speeds to, 17–18, 20–21, 23, 33–36

Mars Exploration Module (MEM), 42, 43, 78, 80, 85–86, 88
Mercury, characteristics, 11, 48, 50, 102–3, 104, 106, 107; expedition to, 101–9, 120–22; lander, 43, 103–4, 107, 109; rotation period, 102, 106; solar day, 106; and solar flares, 91–92; travel speeds to, 22, 23, 35
Meteoroids, 20, 65–66
Meteorologist, 72, 82, 107
Modules, 16, 42, 43; rotating m., 55, 56, 73–74; replacement of, 122
Moon, distance, 9; and training trips to, 46, 48; useful areas, 50
Murray, Bruce C. *See* Davies, Merton

National Aeronautics and Space Administration (NASA), 14, 25, 26, 30, 43, 54, 64, 68, 69; and space station, 58, 61, 118, 119; and space tug, 103
National Geographic, 74
Navigation, 112–13
NERVA (nuclear rocket), 30, 32, 36, 37, 114, 120
Newton, Sir Isaac, 26
Nitrogen, 64–65; liquid, 22, 121
NOVA (rocket), 26
Nuclear isotope-powered generator, 80
Nuclear shuttles, 42–43

Oppositions, cycle of, 14, 90
Orbiting solar observatories, (OSO), 56, 121
Oxygen, 64; recycling system, 61, 62

Perihelion, 92, 104, 108
Pettengill, Dr. Gordon H., 102
Photography, expedition use, 108
Photon rocket, 34–36, 89, 90, 111–12, 120
Photosynthesis, 61–62
Physician, on spaceflight, 72, 90
Planets, 9, 17, 108, 122. *See also* Mars; Mercury; Venus
Plants, 61–62, 70, 76, 108
Plummer, Dr. William T., 85
Propellant, 18, 20, 25, 26, 99; economy of, 30, 114

Quarantine period, 89–90, 118

Radiation, problem of, 20, 30, 32, 54; shielding, 60, 91–92, 94, 101, 114, 117, 121
Ragsdale, Robert G., 33–34
Reentry (into Earth orbit), 114–18
Reeves, Edward, 102–3
Relativity, theory of, 111
Restraints, in space, 37, 40
Rockets, 16, 25–27, nuclear solar, 28–34; photon, 34–36; weight of, 32–33
Rovers (exploration vehicles), 48, 85–86; remote-control, 98
Russians, in space, 13, 14, 118, 119

Saenger, Drs. Eugen and Irene Saenger-Bredt, 34–35
Saturn V (rocket), 25, 26, 42
Schroeter's Valley (rill on moon), 50
Schweickart, Russell, 40
Shepard, Alan B., 43
Skylab program, 53, 64
Solar flares, problem of, 90–94
Solar-powered rocket (SOHR), 28
Spacecraft, 9–10, 114; construction, 37–43; power, 16, 25–33; refueling, 51; replacement of equipment, 120–22; speeds, 18–22; 34–35; tests, 50; trajectory, 17; weight, 25, 32–33. *See also* Crew, Modules, Rockets, and more specific entries, i.e., Decompression, Fire
Space hazards, to crew, 20, 30–32. *See also* Astronauts
Space shuttle (reusable), 119
Space station, 40–42, 58, 118, 119
Space suit, 106
Space tug, 43, 103
"Specific impulse." *See* Fuel, economy

Speed of light, 36
Speeds, of spacecraft, 17, 18–23, 34–35; exhaust, 26; and time change, 112, return to Earth, 114, 116
Sun, gravity assist, 21; gravity of, 17, 18, 19, 23; and Mercury, 92, 104; size, 108
Synodic mission, 20, 21, 89

Television, expedition use, 78, 86, 97, 98, 108
Third Law of Motion, 26

Unmanned probes, 10, 14, 17, 76, 96–98

Venus, 10, 101, 111; characteristics, 12, 94, 96–97; expedition, 120–22; flyby and orbit, 14, 19, 21, 89, 94–99; gravity, 21, 99; inferior conjunctions, 16; manned landing, 98; and navigation, 113; and solar flares, 91–92; unmanned probes, 96–98
View from Space, (Davies and Murray), 94
Voices from the Sky (Clarke), 104
Von Braun, Dr. Wernher, 30, 42

Waste cloud, 60, 88
Water, on spacecraft, 69–70
Weaver, Kenneth F., 74
Weight, problem of, 20, 32, 60, 90, 114
Weightlessness, 20, 53–56, 58, 120; and plants, 62
White, Edward H., II, 40
Worden, Alfred M., 40

The Author

Walter B. Hendrickson, Jr., is a well-known writer in the aerospace field. He is the author of the well-received *Who Really Invented the Rocket?* from Putnam's and numerous other books and articles. Not surprisingly, his hobby is astronomy. Mr. Hendrickson is a free-lance writer based in Jacksonville, Illinois.

629.45 Hendrickson, Walter
He   c.1
        Manned spacecraft
        to Mars and Venus

DATE DUE

DEC 10 '79			
MAY 24 '84			
MAR 10			
MAR 25 '86			
MAR 10 '87			
MAR 4 '88			
MAR 31			
JAN 27			
MAR 7 '90			
NOV 01 2010			
MAY 04 2014			
MAY 08 2017			

GAYLORD   PRINTED IN U.S.A